D0585564

CHEQUERS AND THE PRIME MINISTERS

CHEQUERS
and the
PRIME MINISTERS

D. H. ELLETSON

ILLUSTRATED

ROBERT HALE · LONDON

ISBN 0 7091 1661 6

Robert Hale & Company
63 Old Brompton Road
London S.W.7

PRINTED AND BOUND IN GREAT BRITAIN BY C. TINLING AND CO. LTD.,
LONDON AND PRESCOT

Contents

Illustrations

Foreword and Acknowledgements

In August 1917 it was announced that Sir Arthur Lee (later Lord Lee of Fareham) had decided to give his country home, Chequers, to the nation for use by British Prime Ministers and other public servants, subject only to the life tenancies of himself and Lady Lee – which latter, four years later, they renounced. A chorus of praise greeted this generous and far-sighted action. *The Times* leader referred to it as "a noble idea, conceived with a fine felicity and thought out with true liberality and statesmanship," and a comparison was made with Groote Schuur, which Rhodes bequeathed for use by the Prime Ministers of South Africa. Much was made at the time of the attractiveness and historical associations of the surrounding countryside. Marching with that of Chequers was the estate of John Hampden, part of which said to have been granted to his ancestor, Baldwyn de Hampden, by Edward the Confessor, while very close are the two churches of Hampden and Kimble, at the first of which Hampden lies buried and at the second of which he struck his resounding blow for liberty over Ship Money. Of the connection of his cousin, Oliver Cromwell, with Chequers more will be said later. Hard by is Wendover, for which Hampden and much later Burke and Canning sat in Parliament and where Burke had a country house and is buried. Also in the neighbourhood is Hughenden Manor, the home of Disraeli. It was pointed out at the time of Lee's gift that, as the Prime Minister of the future surveyed this delightful landscape from one of the vantage points on the estate, he could not fail to feel that the whole scene gave an extraordinarily gratifying impression of comfort, competence and peace, which was all so very English, and that here indeed was a country which was worthy of the undying love and tireless service of any English statesman.

As a donor of country houses by important public servants, Lee was a pioneer. His example has since been followed by others. In 1942 Dorneywood was presented to the nation by the late Lord Courtauld Thompson, and it has since been established as the country house of the Foreign Secretary. And it is understood that a movement is now on foot to provide a country home for the Leader of the Opposition. But curiously little information has so far been made available to the general public about Lee, his gift and its results. Lee himself wrote a very lengthy autobiography aptly entitled *A Good Innings*, but very few copies were printed and these were confined to his intimate circle. It is understood that an abridged edition of this will shortly appear, and when it does this volume should be well worth reading, for Lee had an interesting and varied life.

My own concern is not with his life as such but rather with his gift and its results, but Lee and Lady Lee are both very much a part of the Chequers story, and it is therefore inevitable that there should be a certain amount about them in these pages. So far as Chequers is concerned, it is the more recent period with which I propose particularly to deal. The early history (a brief outline only of which has been given here for the sake of completeness) has already been very fully covered by Mr Gilbert Jenkins in his scholarly work, *Chequers: a History of the Prime Minister's Buckinghamshire Home*, which also includes an excellent account of the different rooms and their contents. My own aim is to lay particular stress on the period since the Prime Ministers have been in occupation of Chequers and to give especial prominence to the hitherto unpublished letters which they and their wives have written to Lord and Lady Lee expressing their appreciation of the place and all that it had meant to them. For permission to quote from the letters written by Stanley Baldwin, Ramsay MacDonald and Neville Chamberlain I wish to thank Earl Baldwin of Bewdley, Mr Malcolm MacDonald and Mrs Stephen Lloyd, and in respect of those written by herself, Lady Spencer Churchill. The letters themselves are included amongst the interesting collection of Lee papers to which I was given access and supplied with certain copies by the kindness of Mr W. Hardcastle, one of the executors. I must record my indebtedness to Mr and Mrs Hardcastle for this and much other help and information. The Lee papers are now at the Beaverbrook Library which also contains the very important Lloyd George and Bonar Law papers, to which I have also been given access, and I am grateful to the Librarian and staff of that library for this and for all their help.

I wish to thank the Chequers Trustees for allowing me to visit Chequers and to inspect and make notes from the Visitors' Book, which has been one of my main sources of information. I am particularly indebted to Mr C. F. Penruddock, the Secretary to the Trustees for the amount of trouble he has taken to provide me with the information I needed and for continual encouragement and helpfulness. Mrs Hill, the Curator at Chequers during the time I was doing my research, was most helpful. I would also like to thank the Rev C. N. White, Rector of Ellesborough, for much interesting information. Mrs Fortescue (sister of Delaval Astley, a former owner of Chequers) kindly placed some of her family papers at my disposal and these were a great help.

I must also thank the Librarian and staffs of the Lancashire County, Aylesbury, Buckinghamshire County, New York, B.B.C. Radio Times Hulton Picture and London Libraries for valuable assistance.

I also wish to thank Earl Mountbatten of Burma, the Earl of Avon, the Earl of Longford, the present Earl Attlee, Mr Selwyn Lloyd, Mrs Peterkin (daughter of Ramsay MacDonald), Mrs Stephen Lloyd (daughter of Neville Chamberlain), Mr E. Randag, Mr A. Hain, Lady Olwen Carey Evans, Mrs Cazalet Keir, Mr J. Colville, Mr E. D. Clark, Mrs Carter, Mr Michael Philips, M. Albert Gazier and Mr J. Hewitt, all of whom gave me valuable help and information, as did also the late Mrs Kathleen Clarke and (in addition to the permissions already referred to) Lady Spencer Churchill, Mrs Stephen Lloyd, the present Earl Baldwin of Bewdley and Mr Malcolm MacDonald.

I wish to thank the following for giving me permission to make quotations and otherwise to use copyright material: A. P. Watt and Son (*Field Marshal Sir Henry Wilson, his Life and Diaries* by Callwell); George G. Harrap & Co. Ltd. (*Calculated Risk* by General Mark Clark); Hutchinson & Co. (Publishers) Ltd. (*Men and Work* by Lord Citrine); Constable & Co. Ltd. (*No End of a Lesson* by Anthony Nutting), William Collins, Sons & Co.

Ltd. (*Turn of the Tide* and *Triumph in the West*, studies based on the diaries, etc of Field Marshal Lord Alanbrooke by Arthur Bryant, and also *Harold Nicolson Diaries and Letters 1930–1939*, edited by Nigel Nicolson); William Heinemann L.d. (*Waging Peace*, the memoirs of President Eisenhower, Vol. 2 *The White House Years* 1956–1961); Hodder and Stoughton Ltd. (*The Autobiography of Lord Haldane*); the London School of Economics and Political Science (*Diaries of Beatrice Webb 1924–1932*, with an introduction by Margaret Cole); Beaverbrook Newspapers Ltd. (*War Memoirs of David Lloyd George* and letters written by him); Beaverbrook Foundation (letters written to Lloyd George by Bonar Law); Mrs Ruth Wyndham and *Country Life* (article by Hubert Astley); Lady Griffiths Boscawen (letter written by her late husband, Sir A. Griffiths Boscawen, while Minister of Agriculture); Times Newspapers Ltd. (Leading article of 28th February 1921); Mr Harold Macmillan (letter to the Rector of Ellesborough), *A Diary with Letters* by Thomas Jones (Oxford University Press); Harvard University Press (*Letters of Theodore Roosevelt*, ed. Elting E. Morison), Cassell and Co. Ltd (*Churchill's War Speeches*, compiled Charles Eade).

I also wish to express my indebtedness to the authors, publishers and owners of the copyright of the books and other publications referred to in the Bibliography for the great assistance which these have been to me. Finally I must thank Mrs Chesworth and Fräulein Waber for typing the original manuscript and Mrs Osyth Leeston and Mr Gordon Chesterfield (Robert Hale and Company) for encouragement and many valuable suggestions.

I

The House

A SHORT way to the south-east of the Buckinghamshire village of
Ellesborough there has stood for at least four centuries the house
which is now known as Chequers but was formerly known as
Chequers Court. The main entrance is from the Missenden to
Aylesbury Road, through fine, wrought iron entrance gates set
between two lodges and down a straight wide drive constructed
during and shortly after the First World War and called appropriately enough 'The Victory Way'. It is flanked on either
side by beech trees presented by Sir Winston Churchill. Down
this there have driven, particularly in recent times, kings and
queens, Prime Ministers and Presidents, famous statesmen and
famous generals, air marshals and admirals, men of letters, men
of science and men of business, men whose names are household
words all over the world; and from within the walls of the house
have come words which will be remembered as long as the
English language endures. What has caused this Buckinghamshire mansion, nestling in this quiet spot amongst the Chilterns,
to become the rallying point for the great ones of the earth?
The story is a strange one, and it is well worth the telling.

Chequers is a large Tudor house, built of red brick which has
mellowed down the years, with coigns, string-courses and
window mullionings made of local stone, the whole blending
with the surroundings in a most attractive manner. It stands in
a high pitched hollow some 630 feet above sea level. It is set in
the middle of a fine park, comprising slopes and spurs of the
Chiltern hills and is thickly wooded with beech trees, inter-
spersed with larch, holly and box. There are lovely lawns,
bordered by yew hedges and a beautiful garden.

At the main entrance, which is on the east side of the house,
there is a small porch and an entrance hall, and these lead into

the Great Hall, a vast room which reaches up to the roof. It was formerly a courtyard but was covered in during the nineteenth century. It contains over thirty pictures, including "The Mathematician" by Rembrandt and "The Lion and the Mouse" by Snyders and Rubens. To the right of the Great Hall is the Hawtrey Room, so called because of the portraits of the family of that name which hang on its oak panelled walls. To the left are the White Parlour – with its beautiful white panelling, attractive furniture (mainly eighteenth century) and pictures – and the study, and beyond these are the South Garden Hall and the dining room. A wide staircase leads up from the Great Hall to the Long Gallery, which contains the library. Bookshelves run along almost its entire length, and above these is a row of portraits, including several of members of the Cromwell family. In the window at the northerly end of the gallery are the glass panels containing the coats of arms of the different Prime Ministers who have occupied Chequers since it was presented to the nation.

The late Hubert Astley, who knew Chequers well and loved it, and, indeed for a time lived there, having been a member of the family which once owned it, wrote of it:

Mere words and photographs cannot accurately describe the beauties of Chequers, the ancient house upon a plateau of the Chiltern hills, the entrancing views and vistas over the Vale of Aylesbury, the many walks among the box woods which climb from Happy Valley upwards and from Velvet Lawn past Cymbeline's Mount to the summit of the western flanks of Beacon Hill. Whichever way you go fresh beauties meet you. Down into Happy Valley they are there, up to Coombe Hill or among the beech woods which stretch to Hampden they are there also, and there again when, taking your way along the grass drive which skirts the northern flanks of Beacon Hill, you look across the vale where in the distance lies Mentmore and immediately beneath you the village of Ellesborough with its church upon its mound of commanding position. Chequers is always beautiful, whether in winter when the box trees (and such box trees) are weighed down with freshly fallen snow, or in the spring when the big white clouds sailing in an April sky cast their flying shadows over hill and vale, where lady's slipper and bluebells abound, or in summer when the grasshoppers trill, and when the little chalk blue butterflies flit; and perhaps still more lovely in autumn when battalions of beech are clothed in the saffron and orange of their fading leaf.

The origins of Chequers, like those of many such places, are obscure. It is clear that the house was given its present form during the reign of Queen Elizabeth I when certain major reconstructions and alterations were undertaken by the then owner, Sir William Hawtrey. It is also known that the building so altered dated from a considerably earlier period than this.

The history of the estate can be traced with a good deal more certainty over a long period than can that of the house. The estate is mentioned in Domesday Book (A.D. 1086) from which it appears that "Radulphus held thirteen hides in Esenberge (now Ellesborough) of William I". The modern equivalent of this is 1,248 acres, and at the present day it is rather over 1,000 acres in extent.

Then as now it was bounded on its northern and westerly sides by the Icknield Way, the most ancient road known to exist in Britain, made originally by the early Britons before the Roman invasion and conquest of the island. Overlooking this ancient thoroughfare there can still be seen, in Chequers Park, the remains of what was once the fortified castle of Cymbeline, where his son, Caractacus, is said to have been born in the same year as Christ. It is quite possible that the names of the two neighbouring villages of Great and Little Kimble are derived from the association of this district with Cymbeline. His coins have been dug up from time to time in the fields round about and one of them – a gold stater – is now in the Chequers collection. Again and again this area has been the scene of ancient battles, from the time of the early Britons to the Civil War, and the lines of trenches and covered ways which can still be seen in the park bear witness to this fact.

Within the boundaries of and adjoining the estate are some of the finest viewpoints in the South of England. Beacon Hill (756 feet above sea level) and Coombe Hill (over 850 feet) are within a mile of the house. From both of these, under good conditions, places as far apart as the Berkshire downs, Salisbury Plain and the Cotswolds are in sight, and at times even the peaks of the Welsh mountains, eighty miles away, can be seen.

In the reign of Henry I (1154–89) the estate was owned and lived on by a certain Elias de Scaccario, who was, as the name indicates, connected in some way with the Exchequer. Whether he was a clerk of the Central Exchequer, that great institution of the Norman kings, or merely of some minor local offshoot bearing the same name cannot be regarded as certain. Of the former, Bishop Stubbs wrote: "The whole framework of society may be said to have passed annually under its review. It derived its name from the chequered cloth which covered the table at which the accounts were taken, a name which suggested to the spectator the idea of a game of chess between the receiver and the payer." On the other hand, there is a strong local tradition that Elias was the *ostiarius* or porter of a local building and that it was from this that not only he but the estate derived their names. From this there has been evolved the theory that there was, at one time, a local treasury, and possibly a residence, at Ellesborough, belonging first to the early British and later to the Saxon kings, and ultimately, after the central Exchequer had been established, becoming the property of Elias, giving its name to him and to his descendants and to the estate – 'De Scaccario' becoming, in the course of time, when translated into Norman French, 'de Chekers'. It is certain that the estate remained the property of the de Chekers family until the year 1254, when, on the death of Sir Ralph de Chekers, it passed to his elder daughter Katherine, who married Sir William de Alta Ripa or Haut-Rive, whose property it thus became. In the course of time, this Norman French name changed to the English Hawtrey. It is not known where this latter family came from before they settled down on what is now the Chequers estate, or where the high bank was which originally gave them this picturesque name. There are, however, various legends connected with them. One is that one of their ancestors was a foundling in the Swiss monastery of Altenryf, while, according to another, a knight of the same name struck down Harold and seized his standard at the field of Senlac. It is clear that there were a number of branches of this family who owned land in various English counties in Plantagenet times and it seems probable that the Sir William who first acquired Chequers by marrying its heiress emanated from the Lincolnshire parish of Algarkirk, where traces of a Haut Rive mansion are said to have remained until quite recent times. What is certain is that Chequers remained the property of the Hawtrey family for a period of nearly 350 years, from 1254 to 1597, and that it was during this time and particularly towards the end of it that most of the house as we know it was built.

In the second half of the sixteenth century the main work of reconstruction of Chequers was undertaken by the then owner, another William Hawtrey. He completed it in the year 1565, and it was from this time onwards that the house in its present form may be said to date, though there have been minor alterations and additions since. William Hawtrey made copious use of local materials, particularly narrow red bricks made in the district and Buckinghamshire ashlar stone, the latter being however confined in the main to gable copings and window mullions. This stone appears to particular advantage in the front of the house. Here the line of double transomed four light windows broken by two fine double-storeyed bays stand out against the mellow red brick in a particularly attractive manner, so as to give the whole a stately and dignified appearance.

It seems probable that when William Hawtrey embarked on his major work of reconstructions he made use of the original foundations and this accounts for the present house not being set out on a typical Elizabethan plan. Everywhere traces of his work and influence can be seen. The original glass in one of the windows of the north front had a series of shields comprising the armorial bearings of himself, his ancestors and his connections, and some of these are repeated in the round-topped panels in the parapets above.

William Hawtrey appears to have been a person of some power and influence in his day and age, for, though he never held any official position, he was *persona grata* with Queen Elizabeth I and her ministers. This led to him having a strange experience with which Chequers will always be associated. This concerned the sister of Lady Jane Grey, who had incurred the Queen's wrath by secretly marrying a man of low estate, a certain Thomas Keys, who was no more than a sergeant porter to the Queen herself. Her Majesty ordered that the unfortunate Lady Mary should be placed under close arrest, and the duty of acting as her gaoler was assigned to William Hawtrey. Thus, in September 1565, the Lords of the Council wrote to him that the

B

Queen had appointed that the Lady Mary should be consigned to him and should not "go out of his house abroad, except it be necessary for her to take ye ayre for hir helth". She was to be allowed, however, one groom and a single gentlewoman to wait on her, but orders were given "that she be not dieted otherwise than shall be convenient for her sustentation". Lady Mary was kept in close confinement at Chequers for a period of nearly two years, ending in August 1567. She occupied a small garret on the top floor of the house, reached by a secret, spiral staircase, and this has since become known as the Prison Room. During the time that she was there Lady Mary wrote a series of piteous letters to Lord Cecil, and facsimile copies of these still hang on the walls of the Prison Room.

In the year 1597 there was a failure of the male line of the Hawtreys. William left three daughters, his son, Sir William Hawtrey, knight, having been killed in the siege of Rouen in the year 1591. The eldest of William's daughters, Mary, was married at the age of 7 to Francis Wolley, son of Sir John Wolley, at one time Secretary to Queen Elizabeth and a commissioner at the trial of Mary, Queen of Scots. In the circumstances, it is, perhaps, hardly surprising that the marriage was not a very happy one. There is a portrait of Mary in the Hawtrey Room. This was painted shortly after her husband's death, but only the most meagre signs of mourning are in evidence, and the inscription on the canvas is "One thing is needful", the one thing being, apparently, love.

Mary, dying childless, was succeeded by her sister, Brigetta, the wife of Sir Henry Croke. The Crokes first came into prominence during the reign of Henry VIII, being among the families which profited greatly by the dissolution of the monasteries. They owned land in more than one county, but their chief place was at Chilton in Buckinghamshire. Several of them were eminent lawyers, and at least two became judges. The Sir Henry who married Brigetta Hawtrey held, curiously enough, the Exchequer office of Clerk to the Pipe. He survived Brigetta, living on a widower at Chequers for twenty-one years after her death. Brigetta was interred at Ellesborough church, and on the fine tomb which was erected over her remains it is recorded in Latin that there was "nothing feminine about her except her sex". This fact receives confirmation from the portrait of her which still hangs at Chequers.

Sir John Croke, father of Sir Henry, had had the unique experience of holding successively the offices of Recorder of London, Judge of the King's Bench and Speaker of the House of Commons. Both as Recorder and as Speaker he had occasion to present addresses to Queen Elizabeth, and the manuscript drafts of some of these, written out in his own hand, are still preserved at Chequers:

> To speak, most sacred sovereign, of the great happiness and blessings which by your most gracious government and princely goodness have redounded to this your city, and of our thankfulness, our loyalty, our love, our duty, thereby bound unto your Majesty, is the argument I would speak of, but it is such and so great that were my voice the sound of a trumpet, or had I the tongue of the most eloquent, I were not able to speak of it as I should.

He lived on into the reign of her successor.

> We had heaviness [he wrote to James I] for the departure of our late gracious Queen, who, so long with great wisdom and felicity governed her kingdom as the like in many ages have not been read or heard of. She sleepeth at rest with the kings and consuls of the earth, in the house appointed for all the living, and after a happy and famous reign, leaving a reverent renown behind her in earth, hath obtained a crown of eternal felicity in heaven. We lamented for her, but joy and unspeakable joy in your Majesty by the goodness of God is restored to us.

The Croke dynasty at Chequers was not a very lengthy one, for the place remained in the ownership of this family for little more than forty years, during the lifetime, that is to say, of Sir Henry Croke and of his son, Sir Robert. They were both cavaliers, and in the year 1649 Chequers was sequestered in the hands of the Parliamentary Commissioners. It was soon redeemed, however, a composition having been arranged in the comparatively modest sum of £772 10s. od. Sir Robert Croke did not have any sons, and on his death in the year 1680 the estate passed to his daughter Mary, who had become the second wife of a certain John Thurbarne, M.P., Sergeant at Law. She died childless in 1711, when Chequers passed to her step-sister

Joanna, the daughter of Sergeant Thurbarne by his first marriage. A new line thus started, the estate being finally lost to the descendants of Elias de Scacarrio. Joanna Thurbarne married, firstly Colonel Rivett, who was killed at the battle of Malplaquet in the year 1709. She married secondly Sir John Russell – generally known as Governor Russell, because he was, at one time, Governor of Fort William, Bengal. He was a widower, and his eldest son by his first marriage, Charles Russell, later married Mary Joanna Rivett, the daughter of Joanna Russell by her first marriage. It was as a result of these events that Chequers passed into the ownership of the Russell family and thus entered upon a new and important phase, for the Russells were descended through the female line from Oliver Cromwell, the Governor having been the son of his younger daughter Frances, and it was in this way that the important collection of Cromwell relics, which have been so great a feature of the place ever since, came to be lodged at Chequers.

2

The Russells

AT the beginning of the year 1657 Oliver Cromwell was at the zenith of his power and fame. Lord Protector in fact, monarch in all but name, he lived in a state of regal splendour, dividing his time between Whitehall and Hampton Court. It has been computed that his annual income amounted to the enormous sum, for those days, of £100,000, and, though he regularly gave away at least a third of this to charity, he was able to maintain a considerable establishment and great grandeur with the remainder. His retinue included a detachment of scarlet-coated lifeguards, innumerable lackeys and some fifty gentlemen attendants attired in black and grey uniforms with silver trimmings. But this outward splendour was inextricably bound up with piety and puritanism. Constant prayers, sermons and psalms singing were the order of the day both at Hampton Court and at Whitehall.

At this time, Oliver's youngest daughter Frances, who was 17 years old, was secretly betrothed to Robert Rich, grandson and heir presumptive of the Earl of Warwick. From the start, the Warwicks had been thoroughly in favour of the engagement, but Cromwell apparently had not. He was no believer in the equality of the human race and his objections seem to have been based mainly on material grounds. Frances probably shared her father's views of their exalted station but she was very much in love with Robert. She had inherited a good deal of Oliver's strength of will and, in the end, Oliver agreed that she should marry Robert provided that a satisfactory marriage settlement was arranged. In this latter respect Oliver evidently intended to drive a very hard bargain for, on 28th May 1656, Lord Warwick wrote to his grandson:

I fear my Lord Protector does not mean you shall have his

daughter; his demands are so high in things that cannot be granted, for you know what ado I have had with your father about them. And the more trust my Lord Protector leaves with me the better for you. . . . But, if my Lord Protector insists upon these high demands, your business will soon be at an end, for I assure you nothing could have made me come to half that I have offered but seeing your great affections to my Lady Frances and her good respect for you.

The terms ultimately agreed were that Oliver would settle £15,000 on his daughter, this sum being secured on his estate at Newhall in Essex, once the property of the Duke of Buckingham. But Lord Warwick was to settle his whole estate, worth about £80,000 per annum, with Warwick House and if Lady Frances succeeded her husband she was to receive a jointure of £20,000.

On 17th November 1657 Frances Cromwell and Robert Rich were married. Another of Oliver's daughters, Mary, was married to Lord Fauconberg about the same time. The festivities which followed these two weddings were on a vast scale, and there was dancing in Whitehall to the accompaniment of forty-eight violins. All this gave rise to a certain amount of criticism, such as that Oliver's daughters were "insolent fools" and his 'court' was one of "sin and vanity" and "the more abominable because they had not yet quite cast away the name of God but profaned it by taking it in vain among them".

Frances' happiness was short lived, for a series of cruel blows descended upon her in the year 1658. Robert Rich had never been strong and he fell seriously ill soon after the wedding. On the 19th February 1658 he died. In August of the same year, Frances lost her sister Elizabeth Claypole, to whom she, as well as the rest of the family, were devoted. One month later she lost her father too. Oliver Cromwell died on 3rd September 1658.

Frances thus found herself a widow at the early age of 17, but it was not long before her natural resilience asserted itself. Rich, vital, intelligent, strong willed and attractive she was sure soon to have many courtiers. She could take her pick. The Restoration did not affect her adversely at all, for by now she was thoroughly accepted by the aristocracy. Amongst her suitors was a certain Sir John Russell, a country gentleman with an estate near

Chippenham in Wiltshire. He was soon deeply and violently in love with the fascinating widow, but, at first, she treated his advances with a good deal of coquetry.

> I am sorry you have entertained an affection which proves so troublesome to you [she wrote to him] and hope you will not wonder if I take care to preserve myself from the passion which has done you so much mischief. You are too reasonable to interpret this slighting of you for I consider you so much herein as to make you my example and for your sake am an enemy to that wicked disease called love, because it handles you so severely. I assure you, Sir, I so far sympathize with you as upon your account to be afraid of it, and advise you as quickly as you possibly can to rid yourself of such an uncivil guest. Surely that which unmans you, which torments you with much fear, grief and impatience, which disturbs your rest, denies you the common benefit of air-and so near Newmarket Heath too – and turns all your breath into sighs, must needs be very dangerous to a poor silly woman. You have no reason to complain of these lines because they express as much charity and care for you as faithfulness to myself. You are too honest to wish another infected because you are sick. I hope for your recovery, and if I have not forgotten the content of your last, I think I have more satisfied your own desire, for you were so reasonable as to consider my poverty and so only requested one line.

The more she tormented him, however, the more deeply infatuated did he become. In time she relented and, indeed, found herself being drawn more and more towards him, and it is clear that by the year 1663 the attraction was quite mutual for, at the beginning of that year, she wrote as follows:

> I have received yours, and have only the time to thank you for the great expressions of love I find in it. I will not now complain of you or chide you, otherwise I could take it ill you should, after all that has passed between yourself and me, say whether I am in doubt whether I love you, nor can I allow you to mention so much your suffering upon my account, since I must tell you my usage has been very favourable; but I excuse all such escapes of your pen, as proceeding from an extravagant passion.

On 14th February 1663 he replied, assuring her that,

> It is impossible to express the torture he is in until she satisfies the hopes she has given him leave to entertain, being like a man

pressed to death who cries "more weights" or like those good souls who have had a foretaste of the blessedness to come. He is all . . . flame and desire and conjures her by heaven's example and by her pity, compassion, bounty and goodness, to perfect what she has so generously begun, to abbreviate the tedious dark interval in which he languishes and to pronounce his jubilee and triumph.

The wedding of Sir John Russell and Frances Rich took place on 7th May 1663, and they settled down to a relatively quiet but very pleasant existence, dividing their time between Wiltshire, Newmarket and London. Indeed it is clear, from letters still preserved at Chequers, that for the short time it lasted the marriage was a happy one. Frances went often to London, to stay with her sister, Lady Fauconberg, and both ladies mingled in the society of the court. Lord and Lady Fauconberg had a large town house near Charing Cross.

But Frances' happiness proved short lived for, in March 1670, Sir John Russell died, and at the age of 32 she found herself a widow for the second time. There had been four children of this marriage – three sons and a daughter. Frances did not marry a third time. She remained a widow until her death which occurred more than fifty years later. The last part of her life was darkened by financial misfortune and her whole nature became warped and bitter. Her troubles were largely due to her extreme possessiveness as a mother. She spoilt her eldest son William, who turned out badly, rapidly running through his own fortune and a large part of hers. The Chippenham estate had to be sold. The two younger sons had to go into the world and fend for themselves. The third son John went to India and in the end did well. He became Governor of Fort William in Bengal, and it was he who married, as his second wife, Joanna Rivett, the widow and heiress of Chequers, whose daughter by her first marriage, Mary Joanna, was later married to Charles Russell, grandson of Frances and John's son by his first marriage. It was as a result of these marriages that, for the first time, Chequers passed into the ownership and possession of descendants of Oliver Cromwell. It was to continue to belong to his descendants for about 200 years.

Meanwhile another event had occurred which, in the course of time, was to strengthen the Cromwellian association with

Chequers. Frances' daughter, Elizabeth, had married Thomas Frankland, the son of Sir William Frankland a Yorkshire country gentleman who owned a large house and a fine estate, Thirkleby Park near Thirsk. For many generations, both before and after this, the Franklands had been and would continue to be the leading family of this district. The Franklands were also connected with Cromwell in another way. Sir William Frankland had married Lord Fauconberg's sister, Arabella, while Fauconberg himself had married the Lord Protector's daughter Mary.

Betty Russell, as Elizabeth was generally called, had inherited a good deal of her mother's good looks and attractiveness, for before she married Lord Fauconberg had written describing her as "so admirable a creature both in mind and body" that "Lady Russell will not keep her long". The prophecy proved correct, and her marriage to Thomas Frankland took place in the year 1683, but it did not prove as happy as might have been expected, largely because Lady Russell's possessiveness made her a very bad mother-in-law. However, after a difficult year or two, this trouble was overcome, largely owing to the tact and good sense of Betty's husband. "Lady Russell is so extravagantly fond of her daughter that from a causeless jealousy of being less beloved by her . . . some disorders might possibly have been derived to the family if your son had not managed the matter with great skill," wrote Lord Fauconberg to Sir William Frankland.

Frances died on 27th January 1721, at the age of 82. Her portrait hangs in the Cromwell room at Chequers, and it shows how the years had played havoc with those once attractive features. Her face is lined and the expression is harsh and even bitter, while there is a weariness about the eyes which bears witness to the long series of worries and tribulations which had clouded the last part of her existence. Though, as far as we know, she never set foot in the place, it was through the marriages made by her descendants that the important collection of Cromwell relics which are still preserved there came to Chequers. Some of these are to be found in the long gallery and they include two of Cromwell's swords, one of which is supposed to have been carried by him at Marston Moor; while hanging on the left side of the fireplace is the original of the famous letter which he wrote from the battlefield, containing the words: "God made them as stubble to our Swords."

Frances' grandson Charles Russell, who had married Joanna Rivett, had gone into the army and became a lieutenant-colonel in the Coldstream Guards. He took part in the rather muddled and tedious series of campaigns in Germany and Flanders, to which historians have given the title of the War of the Austrian Succession. His commanding officer, during part of this time, was the third Duke of Marlborough. It has thus come about that, both at Blenheim and at Chequers, the two places with which the greatest of all the descendants of the Duke was so closely connected, a large number of letters have been preserved describing the courses of these campaigns in considerable detail.

The Chequers collection covers the years 1742 to 1748, though unfortunately those for 1745, the year of Fontenoy, are missing. They give an excellent picture of the life of a British officer in the army of that day. Colonel Russell's friends had, like himself, all or nearly all been to Eton, and the picture which the letters give of the life they had led in their various camps in Flanders and Germany shows them to have been men of ideals, actuated by a high sense of honour and duty, enthusiastic in their work, quite content with the simplicity and often hardship of their lives, diligent at all times in the care of their men and kind and considerate to the inhabitants of the countries through which they passed.

Though Colonel Russell himself did not, greatly to his chagrin, take an important part in the battle of Dettingen (1741), his letters form an important contribution to our knowledge of this rather odd affair, when King George II, who had insisted on taking command, rode up and down, waving his sword and shouting out orders to the troops in a strange guttural accent which made them unable to understand him. At one stage, to his great indignation, his horse ran away with him. Ultimately he fell off and returned to the battlefield in a thoroughly bad temper and on foot, undoubtedly displaying considerable bravery. "His Majesty was in the field the whole time and behaved very gallantly and went himself and placed a battery of Hanoverian cannon which was of the utmost service and did great execution," wrote Colonel Russell, adding that,

"The Duke d'Aremburg rode up to him and begged of him not to expose his person in the manner that he did, telling him that he was liable to be surrounded by the enemy and taken prisoner. He answered – 'What do you think I am here for, to be a poltroon?' "

At ten o'clock at night His Majesty was to be seen sitting by himself in a corner of the battlefield, partaking of a late supper which consisted of a large piece of cold meat and a tankard of beer.

In spite of bad generalship, the day was saved for the allies by the great stubbornness and bravery of the British infantry. As to this, Colonel Russell wrote:

> When one considers the well concerted scheme of Marshall Noailles who had ordered a body of men to pass at a bridge on the left where we had lain encamped in order to cut off the rear-guard of the army of which we had the principal care . . . at the same time placing batteries of cannon and moving them all along the side of the river opposite to which our army was obliged to march, playing them all the time upon our troops . . . nothing but the unparalleled behaviour of our infantry and the hand of God could have saved us.

And when it was all over he wrote:

> We are, I thank God, now encamped with our men, and we have great plenty of all kinds of provisions and now are finely refreshed after the great fatigue we have all undergone, lying three nights together upon the ground, two of which were extremely wet, and no straw; and yet I thank God I never was better in my life; bread and brandy was my food and the men absolutely for near forty eight hours had nothing but gin to subsist them. We had but few officers killed considering the great cannonading.

Again and again, during all the hardships and vicissitudes of these campaigns, Colonel Russell's thoughts turned to Chequers. He continued to refer to it in his letters, in which he pictures his children, Johny and Molly, "skipping about among the strawberry beds". "I begin to think it long since I heard from that dear, delightful place Chequers," he wrote on 21st July 1743. "No situation that I have seen comes near to it, and it makes me happy to think that the dear babes are there. I often fancy I can see them tumbling up and down the hills". And In June 1743:

> I am glad you have arrived at that most delightful place Chequers and know how happy Jack will be. Molly will feel the charms of a country life more as she grows older, though the little vanity of dress and desire to see company is too natural to be displeasing. I am glad your brother returns so soon, for he is the life of any place and I shall be surprised if the Adams don't make you the best of neighbours . . . I beg you will let your brother have what beer he likes and any wine in the cellar at Missenden that he thinks won't keep, such as the claret and port. We are still where we were and nothing could be pleasanter.
>
> The plantations and avenues of trees remind me of Chequers. You may imagine Crow Close rather bigger and our camp pitched about half way up, my tent being opposite to one of the cross walks at which I am now looking but also can only in imagination see the dear object of my wishes and the two little lambs skipping about on the grass. . . .

There is no doubt that Colonel Russell and his wife were united by the deepest bonds of love and that they were both utterly devoted to their children. This comes out again and again in his letters, as also does his love for Chequers. In 1742 he wrote from Flanders of "Dear delightful sweet Chequers where nought but peace, tranquillity and happiness can reign".

After the death of Colonel Russell and his wife the Chequers estate passed to their son, Sir John Russell, ninth baronet, the "Johnny" of the letters. He had two sons and one daughter, each of whom died without issue, and Chequers passed from one to the other of them. When the daughter, Mary Russell, died in the year 1813 the estate finally passed out of the ownership of the Russell family and devolved on her cousin the Reverend John Russell Greenhill, who, however, died the same year, being succeeded by his son who assumed the name and arms of Russell, becoming Sir Robert Greenhill Russell. He died childless in 1836, having left the estate to his cousin, Sir Robert Frankland of Thirkleby Hall in Yorkshire, himself a direct descendant of Oliver Cromwell, who assumed the name of Russell. He was an artist of considerable ability and pursued his favourite pastimes of painting, shooting and hunting both at Thirkleby Hall and at Chequers. During the ensuing three or four decades, Chequers was more than once let, not always to very desirable tenants, and at one time he seriously considered selling it. This came to the ears of young Benjamin Disraeli, who was then head over ears in debt, but this fact did not prevent him from looking round for a country estate and for a time he toyed with the idea of buying Chequers. Of this matter, Disraeli's official biographer wrote:

> A few days later (early 1837) he has heard that the well known estate of Chequers Court is to be sold and "we here wish to purchase".
> "I should suppose" he adds in his usual airy way "not under £40,000, perhaps £10,000 more as there is timber; but at any rate I should like to have the purchase money on mortgage if practicable; if not, we must manage some other way."

Sir Robert Frankland Russell did not have any sons but only daughters. He was a very wealthy man, and when he died in 1849 he left his entire estate, including both Chequers and Thirkleby Hall, to his widow absolutely. She in turn, in a will of almost incredible complexity and length (over 50,000 words), left Chequers to her fifth daughter, Rosalind, for life, with remainder to Rosalind's sons successively in tail male. Thirkleby was settled under the same will on an older daughter and her issue. Rosalind had married a Mr Astley and assumed the name of Frankland Russell Astley.

It thus came about that for rather over fifty years, the second half of the nineteenth century, Chequers was owned by two women. Both had strong personalities which they firmly imprinted on the place, to which both were devoted. Hubert Astley, grandson of one and son of the other, has left an excellent description of them both:

> I remember well my maternal grandmother, Lady Frankland Russell, who after my grandfather's death owned Chequers; but I remember her only as a semi-invalid, albeit still ruling with a rod of iron, with a name which instilled awe among relatives and employees. My mother, who inherited Chequers from her, always told us that my grandmother was very lovely, a fact which a beautiful miniature of her by Sanders plainly reveals, and that George IV dubbed her his "pet lamb" which sounds odd (it was really quite "comme il faut" as her initials were L.A.M., Louisa

Ann Murray, third daughter of Lord George Murray). For me she was a little old lady garbed in black watered silk, with a cap of fine lawn at the sides of which were tiny bows of black velvet framing the face which bore the traces of her former beauty. Every evening my brothers and I were ushered into her sitting room (the room at the south east corner of the first floor) to say good night and to receive a small flat chocolate covered with white "tens of thousands". I can see so plainly the box which contained them. I recall how I asked one evening to be permitted to go and read some of Alice in Wonderland which had lately been published and with which I was thrilled and how my grandmother kindly, but to me witheringly, told me before many pages had been perused that she thought she did not care for any more of it. And then the other occasions on which we saw her were when we had to share in her carriage exercise in a big landau, when we generally drove along the road past Hampden towards Missenden, which did not entail going down steeper hills into the Vale of Aylesbury. It was said that my grandmother on driving to church would give orders that the bells must be stopped from ringing when she arrived, as she objected to the clang at a close proximity. My mother would often tell of how she had heard that when her mother, as a young woman, entered a London theatre all eyes would be turned towards her in admiration. In former days she travelled by coach to Yorkshire, where my grandfather, Sir Robert Frankland Russell, owned Thirkleby Park, where he died. An artist he was of whom Sir Edwin Landseer said "an artist spoilt" owing to his not having taken up his pencil and brush as a profession. His pictures of deer-stalking incidents are well known, and two large albums full of his sketches, caricatures etc., always afforded our guests at Chequers much entertainment and interest. There was one of my grandfather and grandmother on their honeymoon, walking along a street in Brussels, as good looking a young couple of English aristocrats as could be seen and the natives laughing and pointing at them, with "Regardez les Anglais" inscribed beneath.

Her daughter Mrs Frankland Russell Astley followed in her mother's footsteps and her son wrote:

In 1871 my mother inherited Chequers, to which she was completely devoted and of which she was completely proud. What numberless times she showed her guests over the house and drove them or walked with them in the valleys on the hills and among the box woods. There was hardly a spot on the estate, however steep or apparently unsuitable for a wheeled vehicle, which was not pressed by the wheels and the hoofs of a pony and cart which she used on such occasions.

It was while Mrs Frankland Russell Astley was its owner that in the year 1880 Gladstone paid a visit to Chequers; he was the first of many Prime Ministers to do so.

Mrs Frankland Russell Astley died in 1900, being succeeded in the ownership of Chequers by her son Bertram. He had married a daughter of the Marquess of Conyngham. He was fond of Chequers, and did much to improve it, but she was not, preferring to spend most of her time at their London house in Eaton Place.

Bertram Astley died in the year 1904, and the estate passed under the settlement created by his mother's will to his son, Delaval Astley, then an infant. Meanwhile Bertram's younger brother, Hubert, had become the Rector of Ellesborough. He had married a widow, Lady Sutton, and they had had a number of children. During a part of Bertram Astley's lifetime and of Delaval's minority, Hubert and his family lived at Chequers, administering the parish and the estate together. Hubert later gave the following delightful description of his time at Chequers:

> There we used to watch the sunsets in the summer and autumn and from there scurry down at break neck pace over the snow in the winter seated on sliding boards or wrapped in sheepskins. There were picnics, too, at Silver Springs where a series of ponds, crystal clear, lie at the base of the amphitheatre, a grassy cup of ground hidden by hanging beech woods with their undergrowth of box, where wood-pidgeons coo and rabbits abound. One hears plainly in memory the soothing murmur of the water running from the upper pond of Silver Springs through an underground aqueduct to keep up the supply of its neighbours who are dependent on it. One recalls the sapphire flash of a kingfisher's back as the bird sped with arrow-like flight across the surface of the water, the banks and woods carpeted with primroses in the springtime, the big trout that lay under the boathouse, the many roach and perch which were beguiled by succulent worms.

A year or two after Bertram Astley's death Hubert Astley and his family left Chequers and the trustees decided to let it. It was taken for a short time by a Yorkshire family, whose name was Clutterbuck; they entertained a good deal, supported the

hunt and gave at least one dance there to which the local
society were invited. They were only there for a short time, however, and in the year 1909 there arrived a new tenant whose
advent was to affect the whole future of Chequers. He was a
rising member of Parliament and his name was Arthur Lee.

3
Lee

ARTHUR HAMILTON LEE was born on 8th November 1868, the youngest of the five children (three girls and two boys), of the Reverend Melville Lauriston Lee, Rector of St Mary's church, Bridport in Dorset, who died in 1870, leaving his widow and young family in extremely straitened circumstances. It was clear that young Arthur would not be able to go to a public school unless he won a scholarship, but this he managed to do – in classics at Cheltenham. Later, by dint of hard work, he won another scholarship at the same school – this time in mathematics.

He had decided that he wanted to be a soldier and passed into the Royal Military Academy at Woolwich. He became a 'gunner' and was posted to Hong Kong, where he did valuable intelligence work which attracted attention in high quarters, and he was thereafter a marked man. In the summer of 1893 he became a lecturer in military history at the Royal Military College at Kingston, Ontario. He remained there for four and a half years.

In February 1898 the American battleship *Maine* was blown up in Havana harbour. Nearly a year previously Grover Cleveland and William McKinley had sat talking together in the White House the night before the latter's inauguration, and McKinley had said to the man he was about to succeed as President of the United States, "If I can only go out of office at the end of my term with the knowledge that I have done what lay in my power to avert this terrible calamity (a Spanish war) with the success that has crowned your efforts I shall be the happiest man in the world." But it was now clear that McKinley's happiness would be denied him. Like everybody else, Lee knew that war between the United States and Spain was now inevitable. As soon as he realized this, he applied to the War office for the position of military attaché with the American forces. In this he was successful, and so it came about that he found himself in Southern Florida during what became known later as the 'Rocking Chair' period of the war. The head-quarters of the United States Army destined for Cuba was the palatial Tampa Bay hotel which stood forth with its glaring, ornamental brickwork and silver minarets in an area composed mainly of dirty wooden houses and in which sand abounded. Men of many nations were to be found reclining in the rocking chairs outside the hotel, sipping iced drinks and watching the Florida horse dealers – military attachés, war correspondents and newspaper men who had travelled all over the world. Uncle Sam was going to war and this event was of interest to his nephews and nieces, his friends and relations and even his enemies all over the world. The old century was going out in style. Many important events would mark its close but surely none more fraught with significance for the future than this Yankee Sir Galahad donning his armour and setting forth for the island of Cuba, prepared for the first time in history to invade a foreign land.

From the beginning, Lee got on well with the Americans. One of their war correspondents, Richard Harding Davis, wrote shortly afterwards:

> There was no one from the generals to the enlisted men who did not like Lee. I know many Englishmen but I know very few who could have won the peaceful victory this young captain of artillery won; who could have known so well just what to see and to praise – and when to keep his eyes and mouth shut. No other Englishman certainly could have told American stories as well as he did and not have missed the point.

When the campaign was over, Davis reported to the New York Herald:

> The only foreign military attaché who advanced with the firing line was Captain Arthur Lee, R.A. He was at El Caney and went with the twelfth infantry up the hill when they charged the fort. The French attaché never got within seven miles of the front. The others were at General Shafter's headquarters, three miles to the rear.

The real enemy of the Americans was not the Spaniards but malaria. Lee himself contracted a severe attack of fever and had to return to New York an invalid; and from there went back home. After a few months in England, he returned to Washington as British Military Attaché. In December 1899 he married Miss Ruth Moore, the daughter of a self-made American millionaire. On hearing of the engagement Theodore Roosevelt, with whom he made friends, wrote to him:

> I congratulate you most heartily, old fellow, and I can't say how much I like your letter and the way you write of your happiness. I know just exactly how you feel. There is nothing in the world – no possible success, military or political, which is worth weighing in the balance for one moment against the happiness that comes to those who are fortunate enough to make a real love match – a match in which lover and sweetheart will never be lost in husband and wife. I know what I am writing about. . . .*

Ruth's father, John Godfrey Moore, had been one of the original organizers of the Union Telegraph Company and had realized an enormous profit on his investment in this when it was taken over by the Western Union. He had then launched out into banking.

His marriage transformed Arthur Lee's existence. John Moore had left each of his daughters a life interest in a settled fund of many millions of dollars, and in virtue of her fortune he was thenceforward relieved of any necessity to earn a livelihood. He decided to leave the army and, on getting back to England, was adopted as Conservative candidate for the Fareham division of Hampshire. In the Khaki Election of 1900 he was returned by a substantial majority. He, Bonar Law and Winston Churchill all became members of the House of Commons for the first time on the same day.

Everything that Edwardian society had to offer – and it had much – was now at the command of Ruth and Arthur Lee. They could well afford both a town and a country house and to staff them lavishly. After one or two moves, they ultimately acquired leases of No. 10 Chesterfield Street, Mayfair and a large country house with delightful grounds and some good shooting, called

* *The Letters of Theodore Roosevelt*, ed. Elting E. Morison, Vol. II, Harvard University Press (© 1951 by the President and Fellows of Harvard College).

Rookesbury, which was in Lee's constituency in Hampshire. Here Lee entertained his friends and gave shooting parties.

In the House of Commons, Lee soon started to make his mark, having wisely decided to specialize on a subject he knew something about namely the army. He spoke on recruiting, advocating better pay and a certificate of good character for new recruits, and his speeches were widely reported and received many favourable comments in the Press. It is clear that both Balfour and Joseph Chamberlain were impressed, and Asquith described one of his speeches as having been of "great ability, marked by wide and minute knowledge".

When Joseph Chamberlain in his famous speech at Birmingham in May 1903 publicly espoused Tariff Reform and a split threatened to develop in the Conservative Party, Lee immediately and actively rushed to the support of Chamberlain. From the moment of Lee's first speech in the House Joseph Chamberlain had had a high opinion of him, and his support on the Tariff issue had strengthened the bonds between the two men. Lee went to stay at Highbury, the Chamberlain home in Birmingham, and was appointed by Joseph Chamberlain to be a kind of 'unofficial whip' of the Protectionist wing of the Conservative party. Lee also formed a close friendship with Austen Chamberlain, and when, a year or two later, Austen got married, their wives also became great friends.

Balfour, not unnaturally, did not look on Lee's activities on behalf of Chamberlain in quite the same favourable light. Lee was, therefore, surprised as well as delighted when in 1903 Balfour appointed him a Civil Lord of the Admiralty. He was, in fact, one of the first of the younger Conservatives to be given office by Balfour. Amongst those who entered the House at the same time, only Bonar Law had been taken into the Government before him.

Lee's tenure of his first office was chiefly noteworthy for a speech in which he spoke to his constituents on naval matters and warned them that the great danger of the future might well come from across the North Sea. But he did not remain in office long. The great Liberal landslide swept him and his party from power in 1906 and it was to be more than ten years before he would again hold a government appointment under utterly different conditions from any that he could have foreseen. He continued, however, to be extremely active in politics and to play his full part in Opposition. He was held in high regard by the three men who mattered most in the Conservative Party at that time – Balfour and Joseph and Austen Chamberlain – and it looked at the time as though he would have a very bright future if and when the Conservatives returned to power. He enhanced his reputation considerably by the part he played in the demand for more Dreadnoughts, and he it was who coined the phrase "We want eight and we won't wait." He soon developed into a fluent speaker and an able debater, and he was remorseless in his attacks on the Government when he felt that their neglect of the nation's defences made such attacks justified.

By the end of the year 1908, the Lees had decided to look around for another country house; the lease of Rookesbury was soon due to terminate. Chequers at that time was to let, and the Lees first saw it in January 1909 and decided that this was the place for them. They immediately entered into negotiations with the Astleys' solicitors, and by the end of February they had secured a lease of the property for their joint lives. It was clear, however, that it would be some months before they could go and live there. A great deal remained to be done. They did not, in fact, take possession until the following July.

Meanwhile there had been considerable developments in the career of Lee's friend Theodore Roosevelt, who had returned from the Cuban War a national hero. He had become successively Governor of New York and Vice President and then President of the United States, but his tenure of the latter office came to an end in March 1909. During his second term, Roosevelt had invited Lee to come and stay with him at the White House, and Lee had done so. Roosevelt would have liked Lee to be the successor to Sir Victor Durand, the British ambassador in Washington, but the Foreign Secretary, Sir Edward Grey, decided otherwise.

Roosevelt's successor was William Howard Taft, a lawyer by profession, who had been Secretary of War in Roosevelt's cabinet. Taft himself had not particularly wanted to go to the White House, but Mrs Taft had, and Roosevelt had added his persuasion to hers and had throughout actively promoted and encouraged Taft's candidature. He had also announced that after the Inauguration he would leave the country for at least a year so as to allow Taft to get well established. Roosevelt had decided to hunt big game in Africa and thereafter to tour the European capitals. Lee was extremely keen to entertain him when he came to England and to this Roosevelt had agreed. Lee knew that Roosevelt was sure to be interested in Chequers because (apart from everything else) of its associations with Oliver Cromwell of whom the ex-President was a great admirer and whose biography he had written.

In the early part of the year 1910 Roosevelt was immersed in the African jungles "hunting the mighty and terrible lords of the wilderness", and he did not reach Khartoum at the end of his African journey until 14th March 1910. He then started on his tour of the European capitals. In April Lee went to see him in Paris, and it was arranged that the ex-President should make the Lees' London home his main headquarters during his visit to England and should spend two weekends at Chequers. In May 1910 King Edward VII died, and President Taft sent a telegram to Roosevelt requesting him to represent the United States at the funeral, which was to take place on 20th May. This meant that Lee had to hurry on with the plans for getting Chequers ready. He was, in fact, able to have his 'house-warming party' there on 27th and 28th May, with Theodore Roosevelt and his wife as the chief guests.

Lee had done his utmost to gather together a party consisting of people who were either already friends of Roosevelt or people he would be likely to find interesting and be glad to meet. The extent to which Lee succeeded may be judged from the fact that the guests included Arthur Balfour, Lord Roberts and his wife, Alfred Lyttleton, Cecil Spring Rice and his wife and Lord Kitchener. Spring Rice had known Roosevelt for more than twenty years, since the days when he had first joined the British Legation in Washington, and Roosevelt had a very high opinion of him. In fact he and Lee were probably Roosevelt's two closest friends amongst the English.

Roosevelt got on well with Roberts but not with Kitchener, who committed the unforgiveable sin of criticizing Roosevelt's

handling of the construction of the Panama canal, which, of all
Roosevelt's achievements as President, was the one of which he
himself was proudest. Kitchener even had the temerity to
criticize Roosevelt's decision in favour of a 'lock' canal, and this
added further fuel to the flames. Roosevelt wrote afterwards to
a friend:

> Most of the time we were in England we were guests of Arthur
> Lee, sometimes at his London house and sometimes at his country
> house Chequers Court – a delightful place. I am exceedingly fond
> of Arthur Lee. He had the most delightful parties imaginable at
> Chequers, just the right people. . . . The only man I did not like
> was Kitchener. He is a strong man but exceedingly bumptious and
> everlastingly posing as a strong man, whereas Roberts is a parti-
> cularly gentle, modest and considerate little fellow. . . .*

After leaving Chequers, Roosevelt went to stay with his old
friend Sir George Trevelyan at the latter's country home near
Stratford on Avon. The ex-President then filled a number of
other engagements in England, but before returning to the
United States he spent another two nights at Chequers on 3rd
and 4th June. He was accompanied by his wife and daughter –
in-law as well as his son Kermit. On this occasion the company
was a little less political and military, though John Burns was
amongst the guests; but the party also included R. F. Scott (of
the Polar expedition), the well-known journalist J. L. Garvin
and the historical writer F. S. Oliver, whose *Life of Alexander
Hamilton* had greatly interested Roosevelt. When he left,
Roosevelt distributed a number of gold sovereigns amongst the
members of the staff.

There is no doubt that Roosevelt thoroughly enjoyed himself
at Chequers, about which, when he got back to America, he
wrote to Lee telling him that "the memories of my stay with you
grow brighter and brighter. The days . . . especially at Chequers
will always remain in our minds as fraught with the best of all
possible associations. . . ." And in other letters he wrote: "Our
stay with you in London and even more at Chequers was a
practically unalloyed delight." And: "those days we spent in
your two houses, but especially at Chequers we will always look

* *The Letters of Theodore Roosevelt*, ed. Elting E. Morison, Vol. VII, Harvard
University Press (1954).

back to as being really delightful. You had just the men we wanted to see and we were with the host and hostess whom we desired to be with." And to F. S. Oliver, Roosevelt wrote when he got back to America: "One of the memories of my English stay which I shall always prize is the visit we made together at Chequers".*

One of Lee's first actions after the lease of Chequers had been signed was to secure the services of a whole-time engineer who was to be responsible for the very considerable alterations and improvements which he had decided to make. At that time the public services which have since become available did not exist, and the owners and occupiers of places like Chequers had to rely entirely on their own efforts and resources for heating, lighting, water supplies, etc. Lee immediately started to install electric light (including his own generating plant), a modern sewage system and an entirely new system for the supply of water. This latter involved the construction at first of one and later of two reservoirs in the grounds. Modern plumbing arrangements were initiated, and these included a number of new bathrooms. The staff at Chequers when the Lees had become established there included two chauffeurs, six gardeners, a butler and a footman, a valet, two odd job men, a cook, a kitchen maid, two house-maids, two parlour maids and Lady Lee's own maid. But though extremely wealthy and though they lived comfortably and entertained well, the Lees never spent money in ways in which many people in their position would have spent it. Thus Lee neither hunted nor shot at Chequers, though the local hunt was occasionally allowed to meet there. The Lees never attempted by lavish entertainment of their neighbours to achieve a great position in the county. Oddly enough, in spite of its long history and the distinguished people who have been there, Chequers has never been a particularly prominent centre for local functions. Then as now its visitors came from London and from other parts of England – and the world.

During the period of rather over five years between his taking possession and the outbreak of war, Lee worked wonders at Chequers. Outside, his numerous alterations and additions included the completion of the work, already begun by Bertram

* *Ibid.*

Astley, of removing the ugly Victorian stucco and restoring the original Tudor brickwork to the light of day. Inside, the house was almost entirely refurnished and redecorated, Lee's object being to recreate the Elizabethan atmosphere, and in this he succeeded brilliantly, particularly in the dining room where he installed the beautiful seventeenth-century oak panelling. The gardens were in an extremely rough state when he took over. He invoked expert advice and the beautiful north and south gardens as they exist at the present day, blending as they do so charmingly with the landscape and the house, are very largely due to the work which was done by Lee and his advisers.

Lee's guests at Chequers during these five years included (apart from the Roosevelts) such well-known people as the Austen Chamberlains, Bonar Law and the Northcliffes. In November 1911 Bonar Law was elected leader of the Conservative Party in succession to Arthur Balfour. This was unfortunate from Lee's point of view because Bonar Law thoroughly disliked him, and the visit to Chequers (in November 1912) does not seem to have done anything to mollify him. The feelings of dislike were quite mutual. Bonar Law and Lee were completely antipathetic. With the Austen Chamberlains and the Northcliffes, on the other hand, the Lee's were then on the very best of terms, though Lee and Northcliffe fell out later on. At that time they had a common interest in flying. Lee had recently been appointed chairman of the Parliamentary Aerial Defence Committee. Northcliffe also had developed a keen interest in aviation. So had the young man who at this time was the owner of Chequers.

In that first decade of the twentieth century life in the fullest sense was for the few – the very few – and young Delaval Astley was one of the few. The fairies had indeed showered gifts on him at his cradle. He had money, brains, good looks, great charm, a long pedigree, a lovely country house and a fine estate. Very different had been his youth from that of Arthur Lee. Educated at Eton and Sandhurst, he joined the army but was only destined to stay in it for a year or two. He shot, hunted, played golf, travelled widely and went to Switzerland for the winter sports. One of his great passions was the motor car, and he soon

became a well-known racing motorist. There was another side
to him however, and in between whiles he did a great deal of
serious reading. He wrote to his sister, telling her that he had
taken to reading the works of "classical authors" and the
biographies of great men and women. "You have no idea how
interesting and instructive it is," he told her.

With all these advantages he would have had no difficulty in
making what was known in those days as a good marriage. His
mother wanted him to do so, but Delaval had other ideas. The
lady of his choice was a certain Miss May Kinder, a young
American actress who had appeared in a number of popular
shows including *The Arcadians*, *The Dollar Princess*, *The Merry
Widow* and *Peter Pan*. In the two latter she had for a short time
played the lead. Night after night, Delaval sat in the stalls of the
Shaftesbury theatre watching her playing in *The Arcadians*. At
last, through a friend, he managed to scrape an acquaintance,
asking them both to lunch with him at The Savoy. After this,
matters progressed rapidly, and early in 1909 they became
engaged. They were both 20 at the time. They were married
shortly after Delaval's twenty-first birthday. His mother completely disapproved of the marriage and refused to recognize or
have anything to do with her new daughter-in-law. This greatly
annoyed Delaval, who took his wife's part, and it may have
been this which caused him to bar the entail and leave the estate
to his wife absolutely in his will.

Delaval had studied the science of aviation at Brooklands and
first obtained a Pilot's Certificate in 1911, flying a Sommer
Bi-plane. He had done a number of cross-country flights,
landing on different occasions in close proximity both to Eton
and to Chequers. He was one of a small band of enthusiastic
amateurs, including Rolls, Sopwith, Graham White and
Hammell, who knew each other well, went about together and
were amongst the pioneers of aviation. Delaval flew all over the
country and went to Wales where he flew for Lloyd George; and
it was there that he had his first accident when he crashed against
a rock fence but managed to crawl out of the wreckage. At the
end of 1912 he flew from London to Paris, and after a short stop
there he attempted to fly on to Berlin, but had to come down
near Cologne. In the course of the return journey, something

went wrong with the machine and he had to make a forced landing near Lille. On this as on other occasions he showed great presence of mind and had a very narrow escape.

On 22nd September a flying exhibition was taking place at the Balmoral show ground near Belfast. A prize had been offered by the Irish Aero Club for a cross-country race. Delaval Astley had decided to take part in the exhibition, flying a Bleriot Monoplane. The weather that day was fine, but there was a strong wind. A large crowd had assembled both inside and outside the grounds. Shortly after taking, off Astley carried out a turn at a height of about 200 feet and it was clear that he was in difficulties. He had banked too steeply and was caught by what was described later as a "flukey wind". He behaved with great bravery in a last-minute attempt to avoid injuring any of the spectators. His aircraft lost flying speed, stalled and side-slipped into the ground. Delaval sustained a fractured skull and other severe injuries: he was rushed to hospital and it was decided to operate, but he died before he could be got to the operating table.

At the subsequent inquest the jury brought in a verdict of accidental death with a rider that "The airman, realizing that many lives in the crowd would be endangered had he sought to secure his own safety chose to sacrifice his own life rather than to carry destruction into the midst of the large multitude." Delaval's body was taken down to Belfast harbour, followed by a procession of thousands, the Belfast Corporation being officially represented, and was then put on a steamer bound for England. The funeral was at Ellesborough Church a day or two later. When nearly thirty years later, Winston Churchill sallied forth from Delaval's Buckinghamshire home to utter the immortal words about "The debt, owed by so many to so few" it was of the pilots in the Battle of Britain that he was chiefly thinking, but Delaval Astley, in a very real sense, was "one of the few".

Delaval's death caused Lee to think afresh about the future of Chequers. Though he had not spent much of his life there, Delaval had had a feeling for the place and probably would not have sold it. His widow, however, to whom he had left everything, including Chequers, had no such feeling and would clearly sell as soon as she could. It was this fact which gave Lee's thoughts a new direction and determined him to buy the place and the estate outright, if he could, with the idea that ultimately it should become the country home of England's Prime Ministers.

4

Europe Goes to War
and Lee Makes a Gift

EARLY in 1914 Chequers received a visit from one who, in the
fullness of time, would get to know the place extremely well –
one of those future Prime Ministers for whose benefit Lee was
even now making plans about the future of Chequers. Ramsay
MacDonald, recently elected to the leadership of the Labour
Party, had written to Lee asking permission for himself and his
two sons to go for a walk in Chequers Park. Lee had agreed and
had invited them to lunch.

Born in a two-roomed cottage in the Scottish fishing village
of Lossiemouth James Ramsay MacDonald was the illegitimate
son of a farm labourer and a domestic servant. His early life was
spent in conditions of considerable poverty and hardship – a
fact which he was never at any pains to conceal. Thus he would
describe how he managed to live on fifteen shillings a week
during his early days in London:

> In the first place I used to buy myself whatever food I wanted
> around the slums of King's Cross but I used to receive my staple
> food, oatmeal, sent to me from home, and I always paid for it. Of
> course, I could not afford tea or coffee but I found hot water quite
> as good as tea from the point of view of food and that it tastes quite
> well when once you have grown used to it. In the middle of the
> day I had a meal at Pearce and Plenty's in Aldersgate Street. I
> don't think I ever spent more than two pence or three pence on it,
> although it was the meal of the day. It consisted generally of beef-
> steak pudding. I don't know that there was very much beef steak
> in it, but it filled up a corner and certainly did me no harm. My
> food bill worked out at about sevenpence or eightpence a day for
> everything, so that saving was easy.

He had got to know Keir Hardie and they had become

friends, and this had led to MacDonald becoming the Secretary of the Labour Representation Committee, whose object was to secure the representation of the newly enfranchized working class by members who would owe no allegiance to either of the two older parties but only to the Labour and Trade Union movements. By his work for this committee Ramsay MacDonald laid the foundations both of the modern Labour Party and of his own career. In 1906, at the age of 40, he had entered Parliament as Labour member for Leicester.

In June 1914, Theodore Roosevelt paid his last visit to Chequers. He was there for the weekend of 18th to 20th June, and the party included the Fred Olivers, St Loe Stracheys, Owen Seaman and Sidney Colville. Others who came to lunch or dinner to meet the ex-President were Edward Lyttleton (Headmaster of Eton), Horace Plunkett, the Bertrand Dawsons and Lord and Lady Roberts.

Lee was not in the House when, on 3rd August, Sir Edward Grey made his statement on the international situation which left very little room for doubt that war was imminent, but Ramsay MacDonald was there throughout and made it clear that he opposed Britain's entry into the war.

Shortly after war was declared Lee rejoined the army and went to France, where he held a number of staff appointments. Chequers became a war hospital, and Lee's wife and sister-in-law helped to run it. In October 1915 he left the army, having been twice mentioned in dispatches, in order to join Asquith's first Coalition Government as Parliamentary secretary to the Minister of Munitions, David Lloyd George, who later wrote in his memoirs:

> When Sir Ivor Philipps was appointed to the command of the Welsh Division in October 1915, I invited Colonel Arthur Lee to become his successor. By training he was an artillery officer and thus possessed first hand knowledge of some of our difficulties. I had known him for some years as a member of the House of Commons. He was an able critic of the policies in which I was concerned as a Minister. I recognised his efficiency and intelligence as an opponent. He had taken a leading part in the agitation for eight dreadnoughts in 1908, and I am not sure he was not the inventor of the very telling phrase "We want eight and we won't wait". I had on more than one occasion crossed swords with him

in debate. He was a skilled swordsman, who gave few openings because he had the gift of both mastering his case thoroughly and presenting it forcibly. Early in the year 1915, on his temporary leave from France, he had brought me some startling information as to the failure of our artillery to make any impression on the barbed wire entanglements of the enemy. He was a man of untiring industry, great resource and practical capacity. Although an officer in the army and proud of his profession, he was one of the few whose judgement was not paralysed by an opinion expressed by a senior rank. I found that in every crisis he had a cool head, a clear eye, and a stout heart. . . .

In July 1916 Lloyd George became Secretary for War. Lee followed him to the War Office, having been appointed his military secretary and having been awarded a K.C.B. In November 1916 Lloyd George and his wife stayed at Chequers, but when, the following month, Lloyd George succeeded Asquith as Prime Minister, Lee's name was not included in the list of the new Ministers. This was entirely due to Bonar Law, who had reserved the right to choose the Unionist members of the new government. Lloyd George fought hard and long for Lee, but Bonar Law was adamant – at least to begin with. By the following February, however, Lloyd George, feeling himself to be in a stronger position, invited Lee to undertake the newly created Directorship of Food Production, and this Lee accepted. Of this Lloyd George wrote in his memoirs:

Prothero and Lee were an ideal combination for this undertaking. The former with his great agricultural experience, his tact, suavity and persuasive manner and speech; the latter bringing to his task the same persistence, energy and resource that he had already displayed in his work for the Ministry of Munitions, to which I have already referred elsewhere. The new Directorate became responsible for supplying agriculturists with labour, machinery and fertilisers and for exercising the powers of control conferred by regulations under the Defence of the Realm Act to ensure the maximum production of food.

This work once more brought Lee into closer touch with Lloyd George, for both men were enthusiasts for food production. Lee threw himself into his new work with great drive and energy, and this had important repercussions on Chequers. From the beginning, he had taken nearly the whole of the

Chequers estate in hand himself, putting the farm lands under a bailiff, whose name was Chisholm. When Lee first took over, however, most of the land had been pasture, but he now caused nearly all of it other than the woodlands to be ploughed up. This was a policy which, in his official capacity and with the full encouragement of the Prime Minister, he was enjoining on other landowners and he felt he must set a good example himself.

Lee was one of the first people to see the potential value of tractors to agriculture. Soon after taking up his new duties he started a tractor school at Chequers, where the pupils, mainly women, were instructed in the arts of tractor driving and plough-ing by the bailiff, Chisholm, and the engineer, Hain. Lee was completely relentless in his drive for food production and, certainly during the war, somewhat of a hard taskmaster in this respect, and at very busy times of the year, such as seed-time and harvest, very long hours indeed were worked. The staff, however, were just as keen as he was and needed no forcing. More than once, on clear moonlight nights, Hain and Chisholm ploughed through the night. Indeed, in the spring of 1917, following a long spell of abnormally cold weather, Lee initiated a nation-wide plan whereby the tractors were to be kept going for a minimum of twenty-two hours out of every twenty-four (Sunday included) until sowing was completed.

Lloyd George was undoubtedly appreciative of Lee's efforts, had a high opinion of the man and soon got genuinely to like him. Furthermore Lloyd George was estranged from most of his former colleagues in the Liberal Party who never forgave him for supplanting Asquith. The Prime Minister was now largely dependent on Conservative support and anxious to make as many friends as he could in the Conservative Party. Few men could exert more charm than Lloyd George could when he wanted to, and Lee no doubt felt flattered by and succumbed easily to the Prime Minister's blandishments.

On 6th April 1917 the documents were signed which finally made Lee the owner of Chequers. Shortly after the matter had been completed Lee decided to make known to the Prime Minister his plans for the future of Chequers as the country home of England's Prime Ministers, at the same time however, making it clear that he and his wife reserved the right to remain

Chequers

(*left*) The fireplace in the Long Gallery. Two of Oliver Cromwell's swords, one carried at Marston Moor, are on the mantelpiece
(*below*) The dining room

in occupation until the death of the survivor of them. On 29th August 1917 the Prime Minister replied thanking Lee and adding that "the public spirit which the scheme displays is worthy of that which its originator has shown in all my many dealings with him".

Lee wrote a memorandum, giving his ideas concrete form. This was as follows:

> The purpose of this Trust is that the owners of the Chequers Estate, with the mansion house and everything it contains, shall be transferred forthwith as a free gift (in trust) to the nation on the conditions that: The present owners may (if they so desire) remain in occupation, as tenants of the Trust, so long as they may live and that after their death the house will be used and maintained in . . . perpetuity as the official country residence of the British Prime Minister.

The original intention had been to settle the estate by will but, to guard against accidents and to make the gift irrevocable, it was decided to convey the whole property by Deed to the Trustees without further delay.

Objects of the Scheme

This scheme is not a mere whim, but a carefully thought out policy based upon a long experience of political life and official conditions and of the beneficial effect that the climate and atmosphere of Chequers invariably exercise upon hard working men of affairs.

It is not possible to foresee or foretell from what classes or conditions of life the future wielders of power in this country will be drawn. Some may be, as in the past, men of wealth and famous descent, some may belong to the world of trade and business; others may spring from the ranks of the manual toilers. To none of them, in the midst of their strenuous and responsible labours, could the spirit and atmosphere of Chequers do anything but good. To the City bred man especially the periodic contact with the most typical rural life would create and preserve a just sense of proportion between the claims of town and country. To the revolutionary statesman, the antiquity and calm tenacity of Chequers and its annals might suggest some saving virtues in the continuity of English history and exercise a check upon too vast upheavals. . . .

Apart from these subtle influences, the better the health of our rulers, the more sanely will they rule and the inducement to spend two days a week in the high and pure air of the Chiltern hills and

D

woods will, it is hoped, result in a real advantage to the nation as
well as to its chosen leaders.

The main features of the scheme are therefore designed not
merely to make Chequers available as the official residence of the
Prime Minister of the day, but to tempt him to visit it regularly
and to make it possible for him to live there even if his income
should be limited to his salary.

With this object, a sufficient endowment is provided to cover the
cost of a permanent nucleus staff of servants, of keeping up the
gardens and grounds, of maintenance and repairs and other
necessary out-goings. There is also a "residential" allowance for
the occupant calculated in a fashion deliberately designed to
encourage regular weekend visits.

Lee declared that it was intended that the Trust should last
in perpetuity and that for this reason the following should be
'ex officio' Trustees, namely: the Prime Minister, the Speaker
of the House of Commons, the Foreign Secretary, the Chancellor of the Exchequer, the President of the Board of Agriculture, the First Commissioner of Works, the Chairman of the
Executive Committee of the National Trust and the Director of
the National Gallery. It was also stipulated that, in the event of
any Prime Minister not wishing to use the place, it should then,
in view of the association of the Office of Chancellor of the
Exchequer with the estate, be made available for him. In the
event of neither the Prime Minister nor the Chancellor of the
Exchequer wanting it, then it should be made available to the
Foreign Secretary, the United States Ambassador, the Speaker
of the House of Commons, the Minister of Agriculture, the First
Lord of the Admiralty, the Secretary of War and the First
Commissioner of Works, in that order.

The Lees' decision to hand over Chequers to the nation was
made public in October 1917. It so happened that, the same
month, M. Painlevé, the French Prime Minister, came to
England, accompanied by M. Franklin Bouillon for talks with
the British Government. Hearing that they were about to come,
Lee suggested to Lloyd George that they should all come to
Chequers and that the talks should take place there. He claimed
later that, at what he called 'The First Chequers Conference', the
principle of unity of command was decided on and agreed to for
the first time, and he actually caused an entry to be made in the

visitors' book to this effect. This, however, requires some qualification. The fact is that the so called Chequers Conference was only one of several meetings between the allied leaders at which either unity of command or a supreme allied council or something like one or other of them was either discussed, made the subject of propaganda, intrigued about or used as an opportunity for intrigue. The principle of unity of command was not definitely decided on until the conference at Doullens on 26th March 1918, when the participants on the French side were M. Poincare, M. Clemenceau, M. Loucheur and Generals Foch and Petain, and on the British side Lord Milner, Field Marshall Sir Douglas Haig and Generals Sir H. Wilson, Sir H. Lawrence and A. A. Montgomery.

The meeting at Chequers took place on 13th and 14th October 1917. The party consisted of Lloyd George, Balfour, Smuts, Lee, Hankey, Painlevé, Franklin Bouillon, Foch and Helbronner. Paul Painlevé, the first but not the last French Prime Minister to come to Chequers, had held that office for less than a month (since 13th September). By profession he was a professor of mathematics and had evinced a keen interest in aviation. Entering politics he had become Minister of Public Instruction, charged with putting into effect interesting inventions likely to be helpful for national defence. Later he became War Minister, and it was in this capacity that he had nominated Petain Commander-in-Chief and Foch, Chief of Staff. Ever since he became Prime Minister he was bombarded with 'Interpellations' by his political opponents, particularly Clemenceau, who also attacked him in his newspaper *L'homme Encheiné*. On 13th November 1917, he was forced to resign by a vote in the French chamber and was succeeded by Clemenceau.

Painlevé, who was in an extremely distraught state, did not sleep at Chequers but left with Helbronner after dinner on the Saturday evening. The following morning, Lloyd George, Balfour, Smuts, Franklin Bouillon, Foch and Hankey had another long discussion in the long gallery, and the party dispersed after lunch. Before leaving, Foch, who had been told of the Lees' plans for the future of the place, wrote in the visitors' book: "*Les affaires de l'Angleterre iront encore mieux quand son Premier Ministre pourra se reposer à Chequers.*"

In due course it was decided to incorporate the provisions on which Lee had decided in an Act of Parliament. Moving the second reading of the Chequers Estate Bill in the House of Lords, Lord Curzon said:

How appropriate is the gift for the purpose for which it is intended! Standing in one of the most romantic sites in the Home Counties, amid typical English scenery, within easy reach of London, itself an example of the most characteristic period of English architecture, consecrated by historic memories, repaired and embellished with refined taste, stored with priceless objects, and invested with every amenity that natural beauty or cultured taste can supply – this is a unique possession for which the nation will be grateful and for which its future occupants will be more grateful still. As the Prime Ministers of the future, at the end of a week of toil, fly away from the *fumum et opes strepitumque Romae* and go down to this charming spot they will forget in that favoured retreat Parliament and Cabinets and what the late Lord Lytton so wittily described as "the despotism of red boxes, tempered only by the occasional loss of keys" and they will be tempted, I am sure, to exclaim, in the words of the famous Persian couplet inscribed over the marble arches in the beautiful Hall of Private Audience at Delhi, "If there is a paradise on earth it is here, it is here, it is here."

Lee did splendid work as Director of Food Production. In his drive to increase the nation's food supplies, particularly corn, he was utterly ruthless and untiring. He cared nothing for the feelings or opinions of anybody but the Prime Minister, and his methods aroused the animosity of certain powerful Tory landlords, who succeeded in making things difficult for him, and dissension arose between himself and the Minister, Prothero. The upshot of it all was that in July 1918 Lee resigned from the Government. Of this Lloyd George wrote:

Sir Arthur Lee . . . felt so keenly the blow to his plans by the rebellious Peers that he resigned his post of Director General of the Department rather than share responsibility for abandoning the new programme he had drawn up for 1919. I accepted this resignation with sincere regret, not only because I entirely approved of the Lee programme, but because I appreciated the rare ability and the drive with which Sir Arthur Lee had served his country over both munitions and food production. . . .

Lee spent the rest of the war farming at Chequers. In September

1918 he received a peerage and became Lord Lee of Fareham. Roosevelt wrote congratulating him and saying that this was "a bully title".

When Lloyd George formed his second Coalition Government history repeated itself so far as Lee was concerned. Once more he found that his name was not included in the new Ministry. Once more Bonar Law had barred the way. But, again, Lloyd George was determined to bring him back as soon as he could, and he thought that he saw an opportunity when, early in 1919, it became known that R. E. Prothero, the President of the Board of Agriculture, was about to resign. It seems clear that Lloyd George favoured appointing Lee at once and that, with this in mind, he approached Bonar Law, who seemed at first willing reluctantly to agree. "I do not like the idea of Lee," Law wrote to Lloyd George on 12th April 1919. "It would be a very unpopular appointment but, of course, if he can do the work and no one else is available it will have to be done."

A few weeks later, however, on 29th May, Bonar Law again wrote to Lloyd George:

> I am certain Lee will not do. The suggestion was in the papers yesterday and there was a perfect avalanche of people objecting including . . . the chairman of the Agricultural Committee in the House of Commons. I wonder whether Boscawen would not be as good as we could get. He has done much better than I expected and I believe would be as good as Lee taking into account the unpopularity of the latter.

There can be no question that Lloyd George had a very high regard for Lee, and he decided to persevere. In the end he was successful and Bonar Law capitulated. Lee became Minister of Agriculture in August 1919.

The strength of the friendship which had by now grown up between Lee and Lloyd George receives further confirmation from the very valuable collection of Lloyd George papers, made available to scholars and historians by the generosity of Lord Beaverbrook. These show that Lee felt justified in writing to Lloyd George from time to time about government appointments and his own qualifications for filling them. In the summer of 1920 it became known that before long a new Viceroy of India would have to be appointed in place of Lord Chelmsford,

who was due to return to England in the spring of 1921. Lee
wrote to Lloyd George at some length, setting out in detail what
he considered to be the qualities required by the holder of this
high office and making it clear that he himself would like to be
appointed to it. But there is no evidence that Lloyd George ever
seriously considered Lee for this position. The man on whom he
ultimately decided was Lord Reading, then Lord Chief Justice
of England.

Early in October 1920 Lee again wrote to Lloyd George – this
time about Chequers. In this latter, Lee offered to relinquish
his own and Lady Lee's life interests, thereby making the place
immediately available for the Prime Minister. Lloyd George
replied expressing his "deep personal appreciation".

5

Enter Lloyd George

LEE's hope that the transfer might take place by Remembrance Day 1920 did not prove practicable, and it was ultimately decided that Lloyd George should move into Chequers early in the New Year. Before doing so, however, he paid a preliminary visit, accompanied by his daughter Megan, and he displayed great interest in and appreciation of all he saw. His 'house-warming party' took place during the weekend of 8th to 10th January 1921. It had been arranged that the Lees would remain until after dinner on the 8th when the Deed of Dedication would be signed and, after that, they would leave. The rest of the party included the American Ambassador (J. W. Davis) and his wife, Lord Reading, Sir Robert Horne, Hamar Greenwood and his wife, Lord Dawson of Penn, Lord Riddell and Lloyd George. It is significant that all these men had made their own way in life. Though Lloyd George had many enthusiastic admirers and adherents among the aristocracy, who would gladly have welcomed him into their houses, he did not include any of them among his intimates and neither entertained nor was entertained by any of them if he could avoid it. He could, however, be extremely charming to them when it suited him to be so. Of his guests this particular weekend the closest to him was probably Lord Riddell, who, like himself, had started life as a penniless solicitor's clerk and then, having passed out first in the solicitor's final examination, had made rapid headway in the profession. Soon, however, he had abandoned Law in favour of journalism, becoming Chairman of *The News of the World*. He had also made a large fortune out of property and was now a millionaire.

Several of the guests arrived during the afternoon, and there was a large tea party in the Great Hall. In contrast with the Lees, they were all in excellent form, particularly Reading, who announced that he had been invited to become the new Viceroy and had accepted. Riddell, to whom he confided that he never wanted to see another law book again, described him later as being "like a schoolboy let out for a holiday". At the last moment a message had arrived from Mrs Lloyd George that she would not be coming and so, to avoid there being thirteen for dinner, Lady Lee invited Mrs Clarke, widow of a former Rector of Ellesborough, to take her place. Lloyd George went out of his way to be pleasant to her during the evening.

The dining room with its dark panelling, red curtains, red roses, fine pictures and old gold and silver plate made an ideal setting for this historic occasion. During dinner there was much brilliant conversation as well as gusts of laughter as one witty sally followed another. So loud was the laughter that it was heard by a police officer, named Thompson, who, on that cold winter night and in the rain, was prowling about on the lookout for would-be trouble makers and assassins. As he wandered round the mansion, making his way with difficulty through trees and hedges and flashing his torch into dark corners, he felt that the place, removed as it was by more than a mile from the main road, surrounded by woods and with a complete absence of outside lights, was ideally constructed for assassinations. He was glad when his relief arrived and he was able to return to his snug quarters in the nearby village. When he got back there he found a message waiting for him that he was to call up Scotland Yard immediately. He did so and was told of a change in his assignment. Instead of the Prime Minister, he was to guard the life of Winston Churchill.

Inspector Thompson, as he had by then become, was to return to Chequers with Churchill nearly twenty years later. During his first tour of duty there his main concern was Sinn Feiners; during his second it was to be Germans. But no thought of the grim possibilities which had been troubling the mind of Thompson interfered in the least with the gay atmosphere in the dining room at Chequers.

At the end of dinner, Lee, perhaps to the surprise of most of those present, rose in his seat and started to make a speech. He began by mentioning an old Spanish custom of saying to guests "everything here is yours". The hosts who addressed their guests in this manner did not always, Lee explained, mean to be taken completely literally. Then he went on to add that that night he could make the statement with complete sincerity. In future the house and its contents, dear though they were to Lady Lee and himself, would be the property of the Prime Minister and his successors. The deed of gift was ready and would be signed after dinner. He and Lady Lee had not taken this step without considerable heart searchings and without some doubt as to whether they were doing the right thing, but in the end they had come to the conclusion that they were. He then referred to the peculiar charm of Chequers – its quiet and peacefulness. The house had an undoubted personality which everyone felt who came here. He hoped that the Prime Minister and his successors would take full advantage of the place and give themselves up to its gentle influence. It represented a phase of English life which stood for much. It was well that this phase should be understood and appreciated by those who ruled over this great country.

Lloyd George then rose to reply. More than one of the guests noticed that he spoke, at first, rather haltingly. He said afterwards that he had felt extremely embarrassed. It seems fairly clear that he had not anticipated that he would have to make a speech. He spoke of the trials and tribulations of public life, and in particular of those of Prime Ministers. He said he had read the lives of many of them, and they almost all thought their burden well-nigh insupportable. He considered himself justified in saying that the task of a Prime Minister at the present time was far more onerous than that of any of his predecessors. He referred to the violence and malignity of the press which, he said, made life almost intolerable and made public men feel that they must turn round and claw their adversaries. At this point Lloyd George made a 'clawing' movement with his hands. He went on to say that he believed that Chequers would prove an aid and solace to Prime Ministers in their work. He then paid tribute to the beauty of the place and to its long and fine traditions. He said that, in his early days, he had been somewhat of an iconoclast, but as he had grown older and as he had got more experience he had come to see that it was much easier to pull down than to build up and that skilful builders were the really clever people. Chequers represented hundreds of years of building typical of our great country. That was another reason why its influence would be valuable to Prime Ministers. Lloyd George also referred, in a moving passage to "the healing quality of trees". Altogether it was a good speech, well suited to the occasion, and the great thing was that the Lees themselves liked it and that Lloyd George succeeded in making them feel that he really did need Chequers, that he appreciated their generosity enormously, that his successors would have increasing need of the place and that the sacrifice which the Lees were making, great though he realized it to be would have "a deep, subtle and far-reaching effect on the future destinies of the country".

After the speeches and the party were over, Lee and Lady Lee signed the visitors' book, and after his signature Lee wrote the following words:

> Tonight we leave this dear place, with a sense of loss which cannot be measured, but content and happy in our faith that Chequers has a great part to play in the moulding of the future and that in freeing it for this high task we are doing the best service to our country that it is in our power to render. We are also sustained by the confident belief that our successors here will honour and guard our trust and that Chequers, in return, will give to them, above all in time of stress, those blessings of peace health and happiness which, for so long, it has given to us.

After this, they went into the Hawtrey Room, where they signed the deed of release of their life interests, and Hamar Greenwood, Dawson and Mrs Davis (the ambassador's wife) witnessed their signatures. Then Lee and Lady Lee said goodbye and shook hands with each of the party. Lee turned to Lloyd George and said, "Look after it." Then they drove off into the darkness of the night.

The next day, Lloyd George and Riddell went for a long walk together, and the Prime Minister talked about Chequers. He said that Lee was undoubtedly proud of it, that the work of restoration had been admirably done and that every picture and article of furniture had been selected and placed so as to produce its natural effect. Riddell then asked Lloyd George whether he would occupy Chequers if he were a Labour Prime

Minister or whether he would feel it would influence his actions and point of view. Lloyd George replied that, in those circumstances (if he had been Labour), he would not have occupied it. "It would be inconsistent and would insensibly affect one's mind," he said.

Their walk took them over Coombe Hill and then down onto the Wendover road. On the way back they passed a newly built house, the property of one of Lloyd George's colleagues, Lawson Walton. The Prime Minister remarked with a smile, "I should really prefer that. I would much rather have a fine view and a small house than a big house with no view. I love to see the beautiful white clouds touching the hills. That is what gives me most pleasure."

In February 1921 Lee became First Lord of the Admiralty. This time Lloyd George had no trouble with Bonar Law, perhaps because he (Law) was about to resign from the leadership of the Conservative Party and to retire for the time being from politics.

It has been said that Lloyd George never really liked Chequers – that he looked on it as a museum and was oppressed by the heaviness of the atmosphere and the multitude of art treasures. This is incorrect. It is true that he once referred to the place as being "full of the ghosts of dull people", and he is supposed to have complained that it was these ghosts which made his dog Chong growl in the long gallery, thus disturbing his Sunday siestas. But both Mrs Cazalet Keir (then Thelma Cazalet), who went there more than once while Lloyd George was the Prime Minister, and his daughter Lady Olwen Carey Evans are emphatic that he thoroughly enjoyed going there. He greatly appreciated the comfort with which the staff, who were most attentive from the start, provided himself, his family and his guests, often at very short notice. Above all he liked the walks.

Mrs Lloyd George did not go there a lot. She had public duties in North Wales at the time. But two of Lloyd George's grandchildren were there with their 'nannies' for quite considerable periods and thoroughly enjoyed it. But almost certainly the member of the Prime Minister's family that liked it best was his daughter, Megan. She went there whenever she could and thoroughly enjoyed and was very conscious of the role of hostess.

Amongst Lloyd George's early visitors to Chequers were a number of important Frenchmen, including Briand (then Prime Minister of France), Marshall Foch and General Weygand. The two latter arrived in London on the morning of Sunday 21st February 1921. Briand, who had been in London for some days, was at Victoria station to meet them and, after a short pause at the Carlton Hotel, where Foch and Weygand were to stay while in England, they all drove out to Chequers for lunch. The following day there were to be Anglo-French talks on the twin questions of reparations and armaments. The international outlook had deteriorated considerably in recent months, principally owing to the action of the United States Senate in refusing to ratify the Treaty of Versailles, and for all practical purposes Britain and France now stood alone as the custodians of the terms imposed by that treaty. A leading article in *The Times* of 28th February declared that

> the week which begins to-day will probably decide the fate of the Entente and with it the future of the world. . . . Happily it is within the power of the allies entirely to defeat all German machinations with comparatively little trouble . . . if only England and France are true to themselves and to each other. That is the supreme issue. No execration could be too great for any man who dared to place it in jeopardy.

Against this background, it is interesting to see what happened when the French arrived at Chequers. According to Sir Henry Wilson:

> Foch telephoned to me to come and see me. He recounted his visit to Chequers. . . . He was most amusing. He arrived (with Weygand) at 1 o'clock. Then came *le lunch*. There were a lot of ladies, etc. Then, after lunch they all went out on the terrace. There were 15 photographers and cinema men. Innumerable photographs. Then a walk to the top of the hill, followed by the photographers hard at work. Then a lecture by Lloyd George on the Roman encampments, the cinema going all the time. Then a walk down to the old church, followed by the cinemas. Then a scratch conference of Lloyd George, D'Abernon, Foch and one or two others, nothing seriously discussed; and then Foch and Weygand, refusing dinner and bed, came straight back to dine at the hotel after a futile day which, the old Marshall said, had done nothing except to show of Lloyd George that *"son sac est vide"*.

Briand's comment on Chequers was that it was "*Trop authentique.*"

Lloyd George's occupation of Chequers coincided with a period of almost continuous crises and industrial unrest, and he himself spoke of "one perplexity after another – crises chasing each other like the shadows of clouds across the landscape – miners, unemployment, reparations and, as always, Ireland."

In May 1921 he hit on the idea of inviting some of the miners' leaders to Chequers with the object of settling the coal strike. The Press were enthusiastic about this, and one newspaper declared that "As Chequers now belongs to the nation it would be a most suitable place for a national settlement." Three of the miners' leaders were, accordingly, invited to Chequers, where a long discussion ensued. They stayed all day and thoroughly enjoyed themselves. The Prime Minister took them all over the house, showing them the pictures and art treasures and pausing now and then to invite their opinion of them. He paused for a moment opposite "The Mathematician" by Rembrandt. "There" he said to Herbert Smith. "What do you think it's worth?" Then he immediately answered his own question. "Twenty thousand pounds, at least." At the end of the day it was announced that agreement had been reached, and shortly afterwards the strike was called off.

Lloyd George undoubtedly had plenty of fun at Chequers, and if, in fact, he found the atmosphere heavy, this never had any effect on his spirits. His vitality was amazing. Mrs Clarke, the former Rector's widow, had lived on in the village, and her drawing-room window faced Beacon Hill. Now and again, looking out of it, she would see the familiar figure of the Prime Minister standing on the top of the hill with his cape round his shoulders and his white hair blowing in the wind. Catching sight of her, Lloyd George would wave and then come charging down at a speed which would have done credit to a man twenty years younger, and then she would let him in and they would have a pleasant little chat.

One of Lloyd George's favourite pastimes when he was at Chequers was to take his dogs out for a walk and watch their antics. He was extremely fond of dogs and kept three at Chequers. There was Chong, the large black Chow which used to growl in the long gallery; Riffell, a St Bernard and a little Welsh terrier.

One day, while the Prime Minister, accompanied by these three dogs, was walking through the Chequers woods, the little terrier caught a rabbit and proudly brought it to show his master. He put it down at the Prime Minister's feet and was receiving appropriate praise when Riffell suddenly seized the rabbit and devoured it. The next day they were again out walking and the terrier again caught a rabbit, but this time crawled with it through a hole in the fence which was too small for the other two to get through. They growled but could do nothing about it. "As usual the Welshman won in the end," said Lloyd George, telling the story afterwards.

However serious and harassing may have been the problems and difficulties that weighed upon him, Lloyd George never showed any signs of depression during his visits to Chequers. On the contrary, his mood during these weekends was generally one of lightheartedness. Lord Riddell, who was probably his most frequent guest, has given an amusing description of how the Prime Minister, at breakfast one morning at Chequers, knowing that when he returned to London he would have to answer a number of awkward Parliamentary questions, gave an impersonation of the questioner and of himself replying which sent the whole party into fits of laughter.

Lloyd George did not, as a rule, as other Prime Ministers have, invite either his Ministerial and Parliamentary colleagues or high-ranking serving officers and civil servants to stay at Chequers. Austen Chamberlain and Sir Robert Horne went to stay there in July 1921; Bonar Law stayed there in October of the same year; and in September 1922 there was an important Ministerial house party, which will be described in more detail later. Apart from this, the people whom Lloyd George had to stay were in general his own close personal friends, like Riddell, and people who attracted him and whom he found interesting and amusing. Philip Snowden and his wife went to stay there in February 1922, and in the long gallery after dinner Snowden recited "On Ilkley moor bah't 'at" and Mrs Snowden played "The Red Flag" on the piano. Snowden asked Lloyd George what he thought a future Labour Prime Minister would make of

Chequers. "He would have to change a lot," said Lloyd George. "This place is full of tradition and your people have no roots." Mrs Snowden was again a guest at Chequers from 8th to 10th July.

In May 1921 Lloyd George invited Lee and Lady Lee to visit him at Chequers, but Lee declined the invitation on the ground that to go there so soon would make them too homesick.

During the early part of Lloyd George's time at Chequers, the Chief of the Imperial General Staff was Field Marshal Sir Henry Wilson, who had been Lloyd George's chief military adviser at the Peace Conference. He was never asked to stay at Chequers but paid at least one short visit during Lloyd George's time there. They walked up and down the terrace for about three-quarters of an hour, and Lloyd George seems to have done most of the talking. The Field Marshal found the Prime Minister "most unsatisfactory". He "could get no decision out of him". Lloyd George merely indulged in "scattered talk".

Towards the end of May 1921 the Crown Prince of Japan arrived in England with his suite, and they spent a weekend at Chequers. The Prime Minister took them up to the top of Coombe Hill, and, looking at the beautiful landscape, the Prince remarked "I suppose that these are the villages that Grey speaks of." Lloyd George's grandchildren called the royal visitor, "The Prince of the Pan" and refused to curtsey to him because they thought he was too small and insignificant looking.

In the spring and early summer of 1921 two important matters, amongst many others, were engaging the attention of the Government, and in regard to both of them Chequers was called on to play its part. One was the Imperial Conference, which was to be held in June, and the other was the Conference on the Limitation of Naval Armaments, which was to be held in Washington in October 1921. Lloyd George had decided that the leader of the British delegation to this latter conference should be Arthur Balfour and that Lee should be a member of it. Lloyd George invited the delegates to the Imperial conference to Chequers, and naval matters, including what was to happen at Washington, loomed large in their discussions. In order further to prepare the ground for the Washington Conference, Lloyd George decided in July to invite to Chequers the newly appointed American Ambassador at the Court of St James'. Colonel George Harvey had been for more than twenty years the *enfant terrible* of American politics. Having been largely responsible for bringing Woodrow Wilson to the fore, he had quarrelled with him a few years later and, falling headlong into the arms of Wilson's deadly enemy Senator Lodge, had joined the Republican party. In the manouevrings which led up to the nomination of Warren G. Harding at the Republican convention of 1912, Harvey had played a prominent part, and there were those who identified the legendary "smoke-filled room" with Harvey's suite at the Blackstone Hotel, Chicago.

Harvey and his wife arrived at Chequers early in the evening of a fine warm Saturday towards the end of July 1921. The Prime Minister and his party had been having tea in the garden. So good was the weather that Lloyd George decided to have an alfresco dinner party, and he invited the Harveys to stay on and join them which they did. There were Chinese lanterns spaced out among the trees.

Lloyd George did not use Chequers for the purpose of conferences with his colleagues in the Government or with political supporters and Party chiefs to anything like the extent that some Prime Ministers have used it, but one or two important conferences on domestic politics did take place there during his premiership. One of these was in March 1922, when the Coalition Liberal Chief Whip, McCurdy, was asked down. McCurdy, Macnamara, Riddell and Lloyd George had a long talk in the long gallery. Lloyd George's great difficulty was that he was dependent on Conservative support, and he was becoming daily more and more unpopular with the bulk of the Conservative Party, to the leadership of which Austen Chamberlain had succeeded Bonar Law rather over a year previously. So worried had Lloyd George become over the demonstrations of lack of confidence in him by the Conservative recalcitrants that, in February 1922, he had written to Austen Chamberlain offering to resign in his favour. But Chamberlain would have none of this. He had fallen completely under Lloyd George's influence and begged him to remain, at the same time assuring him of his own unqualified support. In this way Austen Chamberlain threw away his own chance of becoming Prime Minister.

At Chequers in January 1921. *Front row, left to right*: Mr and Mrs Lloyd George, Megan Lloyd George, Lord Reading, Mr Davis (US Ambassador), Mrs Davis, Lord Riddell. *Back row*: Lady Greenwood, Sir H. Greenwood, Sir B. Dawson (later Lord Dawson), Lord Milner, Sir R. Horne

At Chequers in February 1921. *Left to right*: Marshal Foch, Lloyd George, M. Briand

Stanley Baldwin and Austin Chamberlain in May 1923

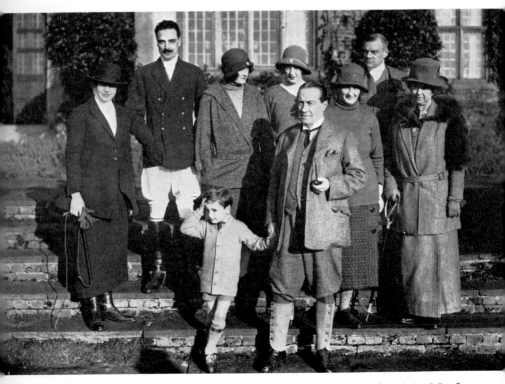

Meet of the Old Berkeley Hunt at Chequers in 1923. *Left to right*: Mrs J. C. Davidson, Captain Gordon Munro, Master Colin Munro (Baldwin's grandson), Mrs Munro (Baldwin's daughter), Miss Baldwin, Stanley Baldwin, Mrs Huntington-Whiteley (Baldwin's daughter), Sir Ronald Waterhouse, Mrs Baldwin

In the course of the discussion, with McCurdy, Riddell and Macnamara at Chequers, Lloyd George said that there were three alternatives. The first was for him to resign. The second was to form a National or Centre Party. The third was for him (Lloyd George) to remain the head of the Government, relying on the assurances of support of the Conservative leaders. Macnamara said the difficulty was the Coalition Liberals. In the event of an election they would transfer their allegiance to Asquith. They did not like the Conservatives. The dislike was quite mutual.

During the summer of 1922, Lloyd George's popularity with the Conservatives steadily declined. Many factors contributed to this, amongst the most important being the honours scandal and the situation in Ireland. Indeed, by the end of the summer it had become clear to most shrewd observers within the Conservative Party and to many outside it that the Coalition could not possibly endure with Lloyd George at the head of it. Then came the Chanak crisis when, in the view and to the fury of most Conservative M.P.s, Lloyd George's diplomacy seemed likely to bring the country into war with Turkey.

In the middle of September 1922 Lloyd George decided to summon a Council of Ministers at Chequers to discuss the foreign situation and also the future of the Government, i.e. whether or not they should go to the country as a coalition. Lee could have attended this, but he still felt he could not face actually staying there as a guest. Instead of him, Worthington Evans, Secretary for War, went. There was no love lost at all between these two. Evans was considerably junior to Lee in the House, but he was a good party man and much more the type to appeal to Bonar Law. He had started life as a solicitor and had done so well that by the time he was in his early forties he was able to retire and devote his whole time to politics. Churchill once described him as "an experienced Parliamentarian, capable of speaking at short notice and of taking an effective part on the spur of the moment in hot debate. . . . He was essentially a House of Commons man." He had a considerable reputation in matters of finance.

The party at Chequers consisted (apart from Worthington Evans and his wife) of Austen Chamberlain and his wife,

E

Winston Churchill, Robert Horne and Lord Birkenhead, the Lord Chancellor. The object of the conference was to decide whether—and, if so, when—the Government should go to the country as a coalition. After considerable discussion they decided, in Austen Chamberlain's words "to play out our hand and dissolve at the first moment the Turkish crisis would allow . . .", and then go to the country as a coalition.

On the Saturday Lloyd George sent a message to Lee telling him that "The Ministers meeting at Chequers desire me to express to you and the Board of Admiralty our warm appreciation of the promptitude shown by the Admiralty in meeting with our requests in connection with the Chanak emergency," and adding, "I need not tell you how much pleasure it gives me to convey this message . . . and to date it from *Chequers*."

The fate of the coalition, of Austen Chamberlain and of Lee was decided by the Conservatives at the Carlton Club meeting in October 1922, when they resolved by a vote of 187 to 87 to fight the next election as an independent party. Lloyd George resigned, and the King sent for Bonar Law. Lee was one of the ex-Ministers who signed the manifesto of loyalty to Lloyd George.

Thus ended the tenancy of Chequers by the first Prime Minister to occupy it. Some twenty years were to elapse before Lloyd George went there again – as a guest of Churchill during the Second World War. Though he did not go there a lot, Lloyd George had taken quite an interest in the place and its surroundings – particularly the farms. On the whole, he had been well liked by the staff at Chequers. He gave an annual party for them and from time to time would invite them to come and watch his film shows. He took quite a keen interest in the cricket team established during the Lees' time but was never himself a participant. He became the patron of the Prestwood (Buckinghamshire) Agricultural show and gave a silver cup for competition among the local farmers for the best carthorse. One of his last exercises of political power and patronage was to secure fresh honours for Lord and Lady Lee. He wrote to them at the beginning of November 1922, informing them that they were about to be elevated to Viscount and Viscountess.

For Lee the Carlton Club meeting meant the end of his

political career and the beginning of a long retirement. He travelled widely, served on several Royal Commissions and was for a time Chairman of the Thames Conservancy Board. But most of his time was spent on his own and other people's art collections, in attending to the affairs of Cheltenham College (of which he was for a time Chairman of the Governors) and on philanthropy. Throughout the rest of his life he maintained a keen interest in Chequers and regularly attended meetings of the trustees. He died in 1946 and Lady Lee in 1965.

6

Stanley Baldwin

BONAR LAW never occupied Chequers; in this respect he was unique among the Prime Ministers who have succeeded Lloyd George. Country houses and country life were anathema to him; he had no affinity with the countryside. The reverse was true of his Chancellor of the Exchequer, to whom the right to occupy the place now passed. Baldwin was a countryman through and through. He had a deep love for the countryside and country people and was never so happy as when striding across country fields or mixing with country folk. "To me England is the country and the country is England," he once said.

The Baldwins paid their first visit to Chequers in November 1922. Of this visit, Mrs Baldwin wrote to Lady Lee:

> We have just returned from your wonderful house and I felt that I must just write and tell you how perfectly wonderful we thought it was and what delight the air of peace and rest gave us.
>
> If it should happen that we are to be the fortunate tenants I can only assure you that we appreciate all the loving care that has been spent in bringing the house to its wonderful perfection. And even if our possession as tenants should be only months we will be able to look back with a happy memory upon the honour that has been ours. Words fail me in which to tell you what I feel about it all, but I felt I must just give voice at the risk of being incoherent.

At some time during the afternoon of Whitsunday, 20th May 1923, Baldwin arrived at Chequers at very short notice. He had left London the previous Friday for Worcestershire, intending to spend the Whitsun recess at his own home at Astley Hall near Bewdley. But late the next day he had got the news that Bonar Law, who had been abroad for the last six months in a vain attempt to restore his health, had returned to London and that his resignation was imminent. During his absence Curzon had been acting as Deputy Prime Minister and Baldwin as Leader of the House of Commons.

Baldwin and Bonar Law met at 10 Downing Street on that Sunday morning (20th May). It seems quite likely that both men assumed that it would be Curzon who would be sent for by the King and that Baldwin told Bonar Law that he would give Curzon loyal support. After this Baldwin left for Chequers, where he remained for the next two days, spending a good deal of the time playing patience in the long gallery. He was engaged in this occupation on Tuesday morning (22nd May), when he got a message that the King wished to see him at Buckingham Palace. "What does he want me so early for?" Baldwin asked his wife. "You don't think he would command you to be in town so early to discuss someone else's prospects of being Prime Minister do you?" she replied. Her surmise proved to be correct, for, on his arrival at Buckingham Palace, Baldwin was invited by King George V to form a government. To the journalists who were waiting for him on his arrival at 10 Downing Street, Baldwin said, "I don't need your congratulations but your prayers."

Baldwin spent the rest of that week in London but returned to Chequers for the weekend to complete the list of his Cabinet. Towards the end of May he asked Austen Chamberlain to come and see him there. Chamberlain had been expecting this invitation for some time and was a little sore that it had not come sooner. They had a friendly talk which lasted for about one and a half hours. Baldwin explained that he had wanted to invite Chamberlain to join the Government but that two or three of his colleagues had said they would resign if he did so, and he had felt that he "could not throw over men who had joined when the boat was very rickety". When Chamberlain asked him why, if he wanted to "heal old wounds", he had not sent for him earlier, Baldwin replied (according to Chamberlain), "I'm very sorry I never thought of it. I'm very sorry."

It was not for another eighteen months that the "old wounds" were finally healed with the inclusion of Austen Chamberlain, Winston Churchill and Birkenhead in Baldwin's second government.

Baldwin was at Chequers for nearly every weekend during the

early autumn of 1923. He was there at the beginning of October, when he spent a good deal of his time making notes for his speech to the Party conference at the end of the month. These show that he was even then thinking of proposing a change in fiscal policy as a solution for the unemployment problem. He was there again between 13th and 15th October, and his week-end guests on this occasion included Amery, Lloyd Greame (later Lord Swinton), Neville Chamberlain and Ormsby Gore, as well as Mackenzie King and Bruce, Prime Ministers respectively of Canada and Australia. There is no doubt that fiscal policy was amongst the matters discussed by this important gathering, and the general feeling, though favourable to some measure of protection, was that it would be a mistake to rush into an immediate election but rather that the next few months should be devoted to preparing the ground and educating the public on this issue. But Baldwin became obsessed by the notion that Lloyd George, on his return from the United States, would forestall him by himself announcing a protectionist programme. It was probably this which precipitated Baldwin into the disastrous decision to seek an early dissolution and an appeal to the country for a Mandate for Tariff Reform.

The ensuing election proved to be the calamity (from their point of view) which many important Conservatives had feared. It cost Baldwin his clear majority, though the Conservatives remained the largest single party. But Labour and Liberals having joined in a vote of no confidence, Baldwin, who had returned to Chequers after the election, was forced to resign, and in January 1924 Ramsay MacDonald became the first Labour Prime Minister to occupy Chequers. The same month Mrs Baldwin wrote the letter of thanks to Lady Lee:

> This first weekend away from dear Chequers I must write and thank you and Lord Lee for all that it was to us. – A happy, happy memory which will last us all our lives and which was the happiest part of the position of Prime Minister. I feel sure that the new occupant Mr. Ramsay McDonald cannot fail to absorb some of the feeling of tradition that clings to the atmosphere; it will make I feel sure the whole Labour party take a wider and softer outlook. As its spirit led you to renounce your possession to give to others so that same spirit led Stanley to sacrifice his position so that he might, if successful, help his unfortunate fellow men. Your example

of giving wholeheartedly we have tried to follow and thought your
sacrifice always of course ours; we feel that we too have given up
Chequers earlier than we need, stimulated by your example of
trying to help others – and though we have failed in our endeavour
we pray that the privilege may be given to our successor. We left
Downing Street yesterday and have come for a few days' rest to
stay with friends before we settle back once more in Eaton Square.

I do hope that you and Lord Lee are having a very interesting
time and we shall hope to meet you on your return.

This is only to say thank you both.

One of Baldwin's last official acts at Chequers before leaving
the place at the end of his first term as Prime Minister had been
to invite the members of the Irish Boundary Commission to
Chequers. They went there for lunch on 28th November 1923
and all that afternoon had discussions, which were resumed the
following day (Sunday), when they again lunched at Chequers.
Mrs Baldwin sat between Craig and O'Higgins, the chief
representatives of each side. "But understand," she said, "I am
not the bone of contention. I am much too plump." When the
meal was over, she went into the White Parlour for her afternoon
rest and found a strange man there, eating a solitary meal. She
recorded the incident in her diary as follows: " 'It's the assassin,'
I said. 'There always is one.' " It was, in fact, Feethem, the
independent chairman. By five o'clock that evening, agreement
had been reached on the boundary and the party broke up. As
they were leaving, one of the delegates said to Baldwin "We had
better travel separately, Prime Minister. To be seen arriving in
London together would not be good for either of us."

7

The First Labour
Prime Minister

RAMSAY MACDONALD arrived at Chequers for the first time as
Prime Minister late on the night of 1st February 1924, having
driven from London after attending the annual Pilgrim's Day
dinner. His guests during that first weekend consisted entirely
of the family circle, and he spent it going round the place,
relaxing and being photographed. Chequers was a source of
great delight and keen enjoyment to him from the first moment
that he entered it. Its beauty, its historical associations, its books
and above all its surroundings made a deep appeal to him. He
became passionately attached to it all and particularly to the
park, with its fine trees. More than once he complained that
these had been neglected by Lloyd George and Baldwin and
that it was a mistake to give too much preference to the garden
at the expense of the park and the woods. Often during his
weekends he was to be seen sallying forth with axe or scythe in
hand to work at some favourite project or to do something to
relieve what he considered to be an eyesore.

After his first weekend at Chequers, MacDonald wrote to Lee
as follows:

> To you must be the first letter I write from this haven of
> beautiful restfulness. They say that Lady Lee inspired you to give
> up this place, and in accordance with the fitness of things I like to
> think that the idea was born in the gracious mind of woman. The
> dignity of stately life and events in far off days, combined with the
> genial comfort of these times, properly embody the thoughtful
> considerations of a good woman (you will pardon my putting it in
> this way, for it is exactly what is in my heart this fine winter
> morning with a gloomy sun outside and the fire crackling on the
> hearth). Only for one reason did I wag a protesting finger at you.

This place will find its way too deeply into my heart, and no reward of public office ought to be so precious that he who holds that office should be unwilling to surrender it cheerfully at a moment's notice. This, however, I can say. Some have preceded me in occupation and many will come after me, but none have held, or will hold, Chequers in greater regard, or find at its threshold and within its walls greater happiness and peace than I shall do. Nor will they esteem at a higher value the kindly donors.

But though Chequers may have been a source of infinite delight to the Prime Minister himself, it certainly was not looked upon with equal favour by important members of the Labour Party. Lord Haldane wrote in his autobiography:

> Unfortunately he [MacDonald] had a passion for spending his weekends at Chequers. When this generous gift was announced in the House of Commons, I rose and shook my head and prophesied that it would prove a dangerous temptation. Prime Ministers who have sprung from the middle classes and are attracted by the pleasures of a country house life to which they are not accustomed are apt to be unduly drawn there. The result is that they lose two days, in each week, in which they ought to be seeing their colleagues and having at least a few of them for a talk on the Saturday and Sunday evenings. It is consequently very difficult for a colleague to see his Chief at the only times when the latter can be readily available. This difficulty has not been confined to the case of Ramsay MacDonald. But with him it proved a damaging obstacle. It was almost impossible to get hold of him even for a quarter of an hour, and the consequences were at times mischievous.

And Beatrice Webb asked in her diary:

> Was the former owner of Chequers quite right in setting it aside for the Prime Minister rather than using it as a home for children or for scholars or for tired and impecunious teachers? Ought there to be such places as Chequers – these places would not have arisen unless there had been a class of persons with the wealth and the leisure to create them.

And in another part of her diary referring to a later phase of MacDonald's Premiership she complained that "The Prime Minister did not ask any of his most important cabinet colleagues to stay at Chequers but did invite society 'grandes dames' including Lady Londonderry."

From this standpoint, a scrutiny of the visitors' book is of considerable interest. This shows that Ramsay MacDonald's first visitor at Chequers (apart from the family circle) was indeed Lord Londonderry. He went there on 17th February, rather over a fortnight after MacDonald had taken possession. Lady Londonderry may have been there too, but her name does not appear in the visitors' book. She and Ramsay MacDonald had first met at a dinner party at Buckingham Palace and had taken to each other immediately. Feeling that the first Labour government must be given every possible chance, George V had taken the unprecedented step of giving a state dinner party in honour of his new ministers. Ramsay MacDonald looked magnificent in his court dress and obviously enjoyed the whole affair enormously, and these facts gave rise to a certain amount of ill feeling within the Labour Party. MacDonald soon became great friends with Lord and Lady Londonderry. He stayed at Mount Stewart, their country home in Northern Ireland, and at their London house. They soon got on to Christian name terms, though MacDonald often addressed her as 'Circe', a name which had clung to her because of a game which she played in which she was supposed to lure her victims into 'the ark'. Many prominent politicians (including MacDonald) took part in this, and she gave them the names which she thought were appropriate. Churchill was 'Winston the Warlock', Carson was 'Edward the Eagle' and Simon was 'Simon the Silkworm'.

One of the things that MacDonald greatly enjoyed about Chequers was the facility it afforded him to indulge one of his favourite passions, walking through pleasant country. The first thing that he liked to do when he arrived there from London was to climb up Beacon Hill. He did this not only in summer but often also in winter. In fact, so persistent was he in taking this particular walk that it became known as 'The Prime Minister's Quarter Deck'. But there were also longer walks that he took. He was no stranger to the Buckinghamshire countryside when he first arrived at Chequers. Several years previously he had taken a cottage at Chesham Bois, and from there, at weekends, he had made his way, shunning main roads and keeping as far as possible to footpaths and by-ways, to some of the loveliest spots and most historic places in the county. He once described this district as "a land of majestic solemnity and romance, haunted by the shades of those who stood for the best in the life of England – Cromwell, Milton, Hampden, Penn, Burke".

On 9th March 1924, Ishbel MacDonald's twenty-first birthday party was celebrated at Chequers. She was the Prime Minister's eldest daughter and had been acting as his hostess both there and at 10 Downing Street ever since he came to power. This fact had aroused great interest and been given wide publicity at the time.

Ramsay MacDonald's guests at Chequers during the remainder of his short first premiership included Alexander Grant, Colonel E. M. House, Edouard Herriot, Lady Warwick and Oswald and Cynthia Mosley. Grant stayed there in May 1924. He and MacDonald were old friends, having been children together in Lossiemouth, and Grant had given MacDonald a Daimler motor car and some money to run it with. Baldwin had also presented a motor car for use at Chequers by his successors. Edouard Herriot, Prime Minister of France, stayed at Chequers in June 1924, the third French Prime Minister to do so. MacDonald had decided to take on the Foreign Office as well as the premiership and had not invited any of his colleagues to come to Chequers to meet Herriot. In their talks MacDonald and Herriot discussed the question of reparations as well as that of French security. Between them they paved the way for the Dawes agreement and the Geneva Protocol. Herriot was also a Socialist and he had been a professor, and he and MacDonald got on extremely well together. They conducted their discussions through an interpreter, but Herriot practised his English with Ishbel and called her his "little English teacher".

Ramsay MacDonald's first premiership lasted for less than nine months. The Labour Party were beaten in the General Election which took place in the autumn of 1924, and Baldwin succeeded him as Prime Minister and, therefore, at Chequers. There was a striking contrast in the way in which the two men conducted the election in its final stages, and this contrast was one of the factors, perhaps the decisive factor, in determining the result of the election. For this was the first time that wireless had played an important part in a general election. It had been agreed that each leader should make one broadcast address before polling day. MacDonald's choice was that his should take the form of a relay of his speech to a mass meeting in Glasgow.

He had decided to make a magnificent oration, to pull out all the stops and to excel himself in denunciation of his Liberal and Conservative opponents. The speech delighted the enthusiastic Clydesiders, but it had a very different effect on the millions of ordinary citizens sitting quietly at home and listening to a political broadcast for the first time. They heard with dismay the singing of "The Red Flag" and the wild yells of the Clydesiders. MacDonald had not yet mastered the art of using the microphone. Sometimes he strayed too far from it so that he was inaudible. When this was brought to his attention he started to shout. He described all those who happened to differ from him politically as "our enemies". All in all the impression which he gave to many of those who had tuned in to listen to a political broadcast for the first time was that of a raving, ranting lunatic. Very different was Baldwin's technique. Shrewdly realizing its importance he had decided to make a special occasion of this broadcast, and he was fortunate in having arranged to get the last word. He went down to Broadcasting House and addressed the nation quietly "as man to man".

On leaving Chequers, Ramsay MacDonald wrote in the visitors' book on 2nd November 1924, "Farewell to this house of comforting and regenerating rest."

And to Lee he wrote:

My first letter was to you and Lady Lee, and so must be the last. I wrote to you as a newcomer when this place first opened its doors to me and its welcoming whispers were still in my ears; now I write after it has become a home and we have been much together. More than ever do I praise you and congratulate myself that I have shared your beautiful gift. Every room has become my own and I bid them all farewell in deep sadness of heart – truly the only wrench which the change has brought. I shall take much of it away with me – the Trustees cannot prevent that! I wonder if it would be contrary to your wishes if I left a book here which would not be disturbing to the peace of the house. I refer to the memoir of my wife. I shall quite understand if you say 'no'.

8

The Continuation of Box and Cox

WHEN Stanley Baldwin returned to Chequers in November 1924, it was still being kept up much in the same way as it had been when the Lees left. The indoor servants included a cook, kitchen maid, a parlour maid (Ethel), head housemaid (Kate), and there were three or four other maids. Kate and Ethel were the mainstay of the household. They were both of the old school, not disdaining but glorying in domestic service, taking a great pride in their work and in seeing to it that the Prime Minister was able thoroughly to relax at the weekends. They both wore the chocolate-coloured uniforms which became a marked feature of the place. In charge of the whole establishment was a curator, but the degree of usefulness of this particular individual varied considerably with the holder of the office. Nearly all of them have been excellent, but there was one who was most unsatisfactory, spending the housekeeping money on racing bets and having ultimately to be dismissed. She might well have been prosecuted if Baldwin, in spite of the false statements she had made about him, had not refused to sanction any proceeding against her.

Baldwin and his wife were both popular with the staff. He himself took a keen interest in the cricket eleven, of which one of his sons was a member, and more than once the Prime Minister acted as umpire at their matches. He also soon became a familiar figure in the surrounding countryside, where his knowledge of and delight in country things stood him in good stead with the country folk. There was one well-known character who lived near Butler's Cross and used to deliver faggots in the winter in a pony and cart. One day he called at the post office, leaving the pony grazing the grass verge. He was kept in the post office longer than he had anticipated and the pony soon got restive. When he came out he was amazed to find the pony some 200 yards further down and on the other side of the road, being held by the Prime Minister. Both were evidently enjoying themselves.

Baldwin went regularly to Chequers at weekends while he was Prime Minister, but, unlike some other holders of the office, he did not spend his holidays there. For these, apart from the annual summer visit to Aix les Bains, he went to Astley Hall, his country home in Worcestershire. It was inevitable that he should be fond of Chequers and still more of its surroundings, for few men have been more deeply imbued than he with love of all that quiet charm and beauty, all those old traditions and ancient peace of which Chequers was both a part and a symbol. And fewer still have been able to clothe their thoughts about these things in better English than he. There was a speech that he made to the Classical Association which expresses perfectly both the spirit of Chequers and the spirit of Stanley Baldwin himself:

> I remember many years ago standing on the terrace of a beautiful villa near Florence. It was a September evening and the valley below was transfigured in the long horizontal rays of the declining sun. And then I heard a bell, such a bell as never was on land or sea, a bell whose every vibration found an echo in my inmost heart. I said to my hostess "That is the most beautiful bell I have ever heard". "Yes" she replied "It is an English bell." And so it was. For generations its sound had gone out over English fields, giving the hours of work and prayer to English folk from the tower of an English abbey; and then came the reformation and some wise Italian bought the bell . . . and sent it to the valley of the Arno, where, after four centuries, it stirred the heart of a wandering Englishman and made him sick for home.

It is small wonder that Rudyard Kipling should have said that the real literary talent "in our family is Stan's" or that Asquith, listening to one of Baldwin's earliest speeches in the House of Commons, should have whispered to the member sitting next to him, "Have you noticed what beautiful English this fellow speaks?"

Kipling went to stay with Baldwin at Chequers a number of times. Neither man was a connoisseur of pictures in the sense that Lee was – none of the Prime Ministers have been that – but they were both keenly sensitive to beauty in all its forms, both had a strong sense of history, and there was much at Chequers that Baldwin could take pride in showing to his cousin: the furniture, the pictures and the fine collection of books in the long gallery. Both had the poet's facility in the association of ideas and the building up of pictures in the mind. Chequers was an ideal place for them to indulge their flights of fancy. Baldwin said that when he lay in bed there and gazed at the Tudor fire-place with the firelight flickering on the ceiling he often pictured Eustace Inglesant's body lying on the hearthrug with the knife of the Italian in him. Baldwin's own favourite reading was Thucydides, but he and Kipling both agreed in hoping that the first people they met in the next life might be Sir Walter Scott and Jane Austen, though Baldwin added that he hoped he might be allowed a really good talk in a corner with Mrs Gamp. Another book which Baldwin liked to read at Chequers was *The Endless Adventure*, a study of the times and methods of the late Sir Robert Walpole, by F. S. Oliver, who had himself stayed on as one of Lee's guests at the party for Theodore Roosevelt.

Baldwin also enjoyed reading detective stories and light novels, or listening to music. One of his favourite guests was Dame Myra Hess, who went to stay there more than once, and Baldwin would ask her to play the piano and would sit down on a little stool beside her while she did so. He loved her rendering of the Gigue of Bach and once said of it, "That is what I would like to have played at my memorial service."

The Baldwins did not generally come down to breakfast when they were at Chequers, but Mrs Baldwin once explained that, whether there or elsewhere, they always started the day together in the same way. "Every morning when we rise," she said, "we kneel together before God and commend our day to him, praying that some good work may be done in it by us. It is not for ourselves that we are working, but for the country and for God's sake. How else could we live?"

Among the villagers round Chequers, Baldwin was probably more popular than MacDonald. Baldwin seemed to them a simple countryman, whereas MacDonald gave the impression of being rather aloof. But Baldwin's simplicity was more apparent than real. It was the opinion of Sir Robert Vansittart who knew them both well that MacDonald's was the simpler nature of the two. He ranked them both high as human beings.

It would appear that Baldwin was the only one of the Prime Ministers during whose occupation of Chequers the local hunt was allowed to meet there. This event occurred in January 1925, and Mrs Baldwin gave the following graphic account of it to Lady Lee:

> I felt I would just like to write and tell you what a wonderful meet of the hounds there has been here today. Everything bathed in sunshine and the house looking like a wonderful gem and shining in its welcome to huntsmen, hounds and pedestrians. – A truly wonderful sight of several hundreds and they all respected the grounds and behaved beautifully, chiefly farmers and their wives and country people apart from the riders; I do wish that you and Lord Lee could have seen how they appreciated the wonder of it all. The Great Hall doors were shut and a guardian outside at the foot of the stairs and only the Hawtrey room and outer hall were used, and now by luncheon it is all tidy as though it had never been, only the happy memory of everyone having enjoyed themselves remains and that I hand on to you – I do hope that you are better.

In June 1929 there was a General Election, which the Conservatives lost. Labour returned as the largest single party, though without an absolute majority over the two other parties combined. Baldwin resigned and Ramsay MacDonald became Prime Minister. One of the last things that Baldwin did before leaving Chequers was to write this letter:

> My Dear Lee,
>   I had it in mind to write to you yesterday and this morning I get your most kind and generous letter which has given me the greatest pleasure.
>   But the purpose of my letter is once more to tell you how your wonderful gift has meant life and sanity to me. These years have not been easy and 1926 was enough to kill a rhinoceros. I owe more to Chequers than I can ever repay. My one consolation in leaving it is that MacDonald loves it too.
>   When I say "me" I mean "us". My wife and I are one in this (as in all else) and in our love for Chequers we never for a moment forget the donors, God bless them!

It was not long after he became Prime Minister that Ramsay MacDonald was walking round the Chequers estate. What he saw disturbed him. He wrote as follows to the trustees' secretary and agent:

Dear Mr Messer,
Will you allow my great interest in Chequers to stand as an apology for this letter?

In wandering about the estate I find what seems to be a good deal of deterioration in it. Rabbits are playing havoc with part of it and especially around the base of Beacon Hill where they are throwing up mounds of white, unfertile chalk, and thistles have apparently not been kept down, so that they are spreading. Some of the trees are dying. I regretted especially to find that one of the firs at one end of Beacon Hill had fallen and the wood had been left in a most disorderly way to rot where it lay. I am told that this is owing to the lack of labour and of course that must be a very serious consideration and it is possible that nothing better can be done. You will not mind my making those observations, however, because I love the place.

There is another point to which I should like to draw your attention and on which I should like to make a proposal. That long straight drive from the eastern entrance – the London one – would be very much improved if it were planted as an avenue.

If there is any difficulty in doing this from the funds of the Trust I wonder if the Trustees would allow me to do it myself? I have been privately making enquiries as to the cost, and other points, and am told that it is quite practicable. If the Trustees were agreeable we could get the advice of an experienced Forester and a friend has offered to supply the trees quite privately from nurseries which he controls. The choice of trees would, of course, lie with you. At the same time I would suggest, if this has not been recently done, that you might agree to my approaching the Forestry Commission and asking them to send down someone who would make a thorough survey of the trees on the estate and give you a report upon them.

I do hope that the Trustees will accept this letter in the spirit in which it is written, and I am . . .

Messer showed MacDonald's letter to Lee, who, however, made it clear that he did not favour the idea of an avenue of trees on either side of the main drive. He and Lady Lee had, in fact, considered this very possibility at the time that they planned the drive, but they had ultimately decided against it both on historical and on practical grounds.

F

Three weeks later, MacDonald wrote to Lee:

I have been waiting to get to Chequers before replying to yours of the 2nd. I was there yesterday and had a hurried look round. The unseemly dishevelment has been removed and the immediate surroundings are far more pleasant in consequence. Would you have any objection to my planting two or three Scotch firs by the two still remaining? They probably would not grow, but they might! My neighbouring landlord at Lossiemouth, who is a very keen forester and has his own nursery, offered to send me any trees that I would be allowed to plant at Chequers. I think the two solitary firs still remaining would welcome a few youngsters round about them and it would add to the appearance of the hill top.

The rabbits have gone. I only saw two this weekend. The thistles have also become more modest, and therefore more Scotch!

I take your remarks about the Forestry Commission as permission to me to ask them to send a man down and report to the Trustees. I suppose I had better tell them to ask their man to see Chisholm so that there will be no heartburning.

I have had another study of the main drive. As a matter of fact some young trees have been planted near to it, and they look healthy and will in time fill the gaps between the beautiful old trees now there. The real trouble is the fence, but, of course, that cannot be helped. I think if a few more were planted down near the house they would not break that beautiful sweep of park which you see when you stand by the rose garden, but would deprive it of a rather blank wilderness sort of look, which its bareness in the foreground gives it. I daresay in the end it is just a matter of eye and impression. From some points of view it is perfectly satisfactory, but if you stand at the study window and look out you see it at its worst.

Perhaps the best thing would be if you and Lady Lee would agree to break what I believe is a rule and come down one day when I am there, say in November, and let us combine our hearts in a survey of the place. I wanted very much to see you before I left for America but every hour gets filled up. You have no idea what this job has been during the last three months.

With kindest regards,
Yours very sincerely,
J. Ramsay MacDonald.

P.S. Of course I know that we can only write each other on the subject of Chequers privately and that the Trustees have the final word.

In the end, MacDonald appears to have decided against the
idea of an avenue of trees along the drive and in favour instead,
of a clump of fir trees on Beacon Hill. In due course he wrote
again to Messer:

Thank you very much for yours of the 29th with enclosure. I had
half an hour's look round the Park this week end. The examination
I made was cursory, but I could not spare longer, as work kept me
indoors the rest of the time. I think you will really have to do some
replanting, and the fallen and decaying trees should be dealt with
without delay. I notice that the oak, planted by Mr. Baldwin at the
front of the house, looks in a very unhealthy condition, but I am
dropping a note to Mr. Chisholm about it, as I am not sure if it is
merely a superficial blighting or indicates something more radical.

As regards the pines on the top of the hill, I never gathered
very definitely from the Trustees what they would like done. The
suggestion I made to them was that they should allow me to do
that as a little contribution from me to the amenities of the Park.
You will remember that the advice I got was that something like
200 trees should be planted on a fenced-in area, which should be
dug up to begin with. As the trees grew they would have to be
thinned out until at last not more than half a dozen or so would
remain for final growth. If the initial cost is £15, I shall be very
glad to find it.

It was Winston Churchill who was responsible for the avenue
of beech trees which can now be seen along each side of the main
drive.

Meanwhile, in September 1929, a further landmark in the
history of Chequers was reached when MacDonald made the
first broadcast to be delivered from it. The occasion was the
National Radio Exhibition. Speaking from Chequers on the
evening of 21st March 1930, the Prime Minister gave what was
described as a "brief introduction" to the radio, shipping,
engineering and machinery exhibitions at Olympia. Six months
later he again broadcast from Chequers on the occasion of the
Naval Disarmament Conference, and this second talk also
constituted a landmark in its history because on this occasion his
words reached out across the Atlantic.

When last I sent my voice across the Atlantic, I spoke from the
Cabinet Room at Downing Street; today I speak from Chequers,
our "Rapidan", but an abode mellow with age and sanctified by

the ghosts of vanished generations. It was given to the Nation so
that Prime Ministers might know that birds sing, flowers bloom,
and body and mind can rest. May I add, before I become official
and careful, that the story of the gift of Chequers may be taken to
symbolise, in the realm of personal affections, blessings of good
relations between two peoples.

MacDonald entertained a number of the delegates to the conference at Chequers. Journalists from all over the world had
flocked in to London to report on it, and one weekend he invited
a number of these down to Chequers and took great pride in
showing them round the house and over the estate. There was a
large tea party in the Great Hall; afterwards they all sat round
the fire and the conversation ranged over a very wide variety of
subjects. So absorbing did these journalists find MacDonald's
talk of literature, travel, the Highlands, the English countryside
and other matters that the conference itself was hardly ever
mentioned.

Amongst MacDonald's very first guests at Chequers in his
second premiership was Lord Thomson, who went there in July
1929. Thomson, who was Secretary for Air, was very different
from the other Ministers in background, experience, tempera-
ment and outlook. He was altogether a most unusual person,
and it was this very unusualness which appealed strongly to
MacDonald. His father had been a major-general in the Royal
Engineers and his mother the daughter of an Indian army
general. Thomson had been educated at Cheltenham and the
R.M.A. Woolwich and had gone into the army, where he did
well, ultimately becoming a brigadier general on the staff of
Field Marshal Sir Henry Wilson at the Supreme War Council.
Yet he was a socialist and threw up a most promising military
career in order to become a Labour candidate for Bristol, when,
in MacDonald's words, he passed "from the ease and luxury of
Paris and the good company of his army friends, to simple
lodgings, plain fare and laborious days . . . eking out his pension
by precarious journalism . . . but finding ample recompense for
all that he had surrendered in the warm affection of his new
found friends of the Labour Party".

Of all the guests whom he invited to Chequers, Thomson was
probably the one that MacDonald enjoyed having there most,

and their friendship ripened and received its consummation in these delightful surroundings.

The names of rather more prominent members of the Labour Party are to be found in the visitors' book during MacDonald's second Prime Ministership than during his first. Between the beginning of July 1929 and the end of July 1931, Mr and Mrs J. H. Thomas, Mr and Mrs Arthur Henderson, Arthur Greenwood and Mr and Mrs Philip Snowden, Lady Warwick and Oswald and Cynthia Mosley all went at one time or another. But there are several important names which are conspicuous by their absence. Beatrice Webb wrote in her diary under the date 22nd July 1929:

> He [MacDonald] asked Sydney [Webb] whether he had been to Chequers; S said no. Then with some awkwardness he (MacDonald) explained that the Trust Deed did not permit or at any rate encourage the holding of week-end Cabinets there; but Chequers was meant to enable the distinguished occupier *to get away from his ministerial preoccupation.* The idea was thrown out by J.R.M. of an afternoon party at Chequers for the Ministers and their wives which Arnold and S welcomed as a way of the Ministers getting the desirable acquaintance with Chequers without depriving the P.M. of his weekly rest. . . .

Apart from Thomson, the one of his Cabinet colleagues who was closest to MacDonald was probably J. H. Thomas. Though alive to his eccentricities and humorous aspects, and though Thomas was never an affinity in the sense that Thomson was, MacDonald was genuinely fond of Thomas and deeply distressed by his subsequent downfall. Another visitor to Chequers of those days was the Princess Martha Bibesco, a most charming and attractive person whom Lord Thomson had got to know in Romania, and of whom he was a great admirer. She was the heroine of his book *Smaranda.* It was Thomson who had introduced her to MacDonald.

MacDonald went to Chequers most weekends, and a regular routine soon established itself. His party would leave Westminster sharp at four o'clock on Friday afternoon, getting to Chequers about 5.30 p.m. They were greeted by Ethel, who had tea waiting for them, and then the Prime Minister was off up Beacon Hill. The staff at Chequers were undoubtedly fond of the MacDonald family, and this feeling was reciprocated. Ethel in particular was full of solicitude and would say to Ishbel in her soft voice if she thought she looked worn out, "Oh, Miss, you do look tired. Do please let me get you a drink." And when later MacDonald's eyes started to give him trouble the staff were full of concern and one of them is said to have suggested that he should not do so much work at Chequers during the weekend, reading government papers, etc., adding that "Mr Baldwin never did."

Ishbel by now was a member of the London County Council, and this, together with her numerous other duties, resulted in her being very hard worked. She was getting about fifty letters a day, many of them insulting, and had all the social side of 10 Downing Street on her shoulders, so that it is small wonder she arrived at Chequers looking tired out, and she too found it a haven of refuge. She had the White Parlour to herself either to work or relax in, while the Prime Minister had his study and Malcolm was generally given the Hawtrey Room to work in.

Breakfast was always sharp at 8.30 a.m. and afterwards the Prime Minister would generally work for an hour or two in his study and then go out either to work on the estate, cutting wood, etc., or for a good, long walk. One of his favourite walks was over Coombe Hill, returning by Great Hampden. He worked in his study after dinner, seldom going to bed before midnight.

On Saturday 5th October 1930 he had gone to bed at his usual time. He woke up early and started to read a book. Shortly before six o'clock on that Sunday morning the telephone by his bedside rang. He had been rather expecting a telephone call, though not quite so early, but the news which he got came as a terrible shock. For it was the Air Ministry at the other end and the message was that the airship R.101, in which Lord Thomson had taken off from Cardington the night before to fly to India, had hit a hillside at Beauvais in Northern France at about 1 a.m. that morning, and that Thomson and his fellow passengers and the entire crew (in all about 100 people) had been killed.

On receipt of this terrible news, MacDonald rushed straight

off to London without having had any breakfast. He got to the Air Ministry before eight o'clock. He then went round to Downing Street, where he received a number of callers, including Baldwin. He had to get back to Chequers for lunch because the Canadian delegation to the Imperial Conference and their wives had already been invited. Harold Nicolson and his wife were among the guests, and when he got to Chequers the Prime Minister had not yet got back from London, but Ishbel had taken charge of things. She told them what had happened, that her father would be back shortly and that he would be in "a dreadful state". This proved to be the case.

It was 1.30 p.m. by the time MacDonald got back to Chequers. According to Nicolson he looked "very ill and worn out". Harold Nicolson's account of what took place continues as follows:

> Bennett, the Prime Minister of Canada is there. Ramsay begins to introduce him to Vita [Mrs Harold Nicolson] but forgets his name. He makes a hopeless gesture, his hand upon his white hair: "My brain is going" he says "My brain is going". It is all rather embarrassing. He then tells us that he dashed up to London in fifty-five minutes. The King was in a dreadful state. Ramsay seemed more worried about the King's dismay than about anything else. The Prime Minister pours out to Vita the miseries of his soul. "Two hours a night is all the sleep I get." He can do no work: "The moment I disentangle my foot from one strand of barbed wire it becomes entangled in another. If God were to come to me and say 'Ramsay, would you rather be a country gentleman than the Prime Minister' I should reply 'Please God a country gentleman!' " He is a tired, exhausted man. Bless him!!

That evening MacDonald returned to Downing Street from which he issued the following statement:

> I heard in the early hours of this morning of the terrible disaster to R 101 and am grieved beyond words at the loss of so many splendid men whose sacrifice has been added to that glorious list of gallant Englishmen who on uncharted seas and unexplored lands have gone into the unknown as pioneers and pathfinders and have met death. My most heartfelt sympathy goes out to their families in this hour of bereavement. Only those who have been associated with Lord Thomson know how much the country has lost. To me no-one can fill his place of genial companionship and friendship.

In the year 1931 Chequers had its first important German visitors. Herren Brüning and Curtius, German Chancellor and Foreign Secretary respectively, were there on 6th and 7th June of that year, a large luncheon party being given for them at Chequers on Saturday 6th June. The Chequers meeting was extremely important from Brüning's point of view. What he now needed above all things was a big success in foreign policy to distract attention at home from domestic problems and to ward off the danger of a further advance by the Nazis. In particular, he hoped to secure concessions over armaments and reparations. Brüning knew that what would be popular in Germany would be a state of affairs in which everyone but Germany disarmed and in which reparations were effectively terminated. Here he had high hopes of MacDonald, who was generally regarded as being sympathetic to the German point of view and easily flattered. But, in his second government, MacDonald had not taken on the Foreign Office himself. Not he but Arthur Henderson was now the Foreign Secretary.

There was a large lunch party at Chequers on the Saturday (6th June) in honour of the German visitors. The guests, apart from Brüning and Curtius, included Mr and Mrs Arthur Henderson, William Graham, Baron Von Neurath (German Ambassador), Sir Clive Wigram (private secretary to the King) and Lady Wigram, Montagu Norman (Governor of the Bank of England), Bernard Shaw and his wife, Sir Robert Vansittart (Permanent Under Secretary at the Foreign Office), Sir Leith Ross, Mr and Mrs A. V. Alexander and Herr Schmidt, the interpreter. Ishbel was the hostess, and Malcolm and Sheila MacDonald were there too. In the course of the ensuing discussions, Vansittart warned Brüning and Curtius that "the question of debts could not be pushed at this end until after the American elections", and he "shared their view that in the meanwhile Hindenburg might fall".

During the time they were at Chequers, MacDonald took great pride in showing his German guests round the house and grounds. There were some captured German cannon in the park, which had been rather clumsily concealed just before the visit, and in the course of their walk Brüning and Curtius dis-

covered these, to MacDonald's embarrassment but their
amusement.

A *communiqué* issued after the Chequers talks stated:

> Special stress was laid by the German Ministers on the difficul-
> ties of the existing position in which the German Reich and other
> industrial states now found themselves and on the need for allevia-
> tion. The British Ministers for their part called attention to the
> world wide character of the present depression and its special
> influence on their own country. Both parties were agreed that, in
> addition to efforts and measures of a national character, the
> revival of confidence and prosperity depended upon international
> co-operation. . . .

The few years that still remained to Ramsay MacDonald were
not destined to be very happy ones. The depression got worse,
the unemployment fund went more deeply into debt, foreigners
withdrew more and more of their balances from London,
sterling came under increasing pressure, and the Government
were faced with the certainty of a serious budgetary deficit and
the likelihood (in the opinion of some) of financial disaster to the
nation unless drastic steps were taken. Matters came to a head in
August 1931; the crucial issue was unemployment pay. By a
very narrow majority, the Cabinet agreed to a cut of 10 per cent
in the rate of benefit, but a number of very important Labour
Ministers (including Henderson, Clynes and Graham) refused
to agree to any cut at all. MacDonald felt that in view of this
serious division of opinion it was impossible for the Labour
government to continue. His colleagues agreed with him about
this and handed him their resignations. They assumed that
Baldwin would now be invited to form a government.

It was late on the evening of Sunday 23rd August when
Ramsay MacDonald arrived at the Palace, carrying with him
in his pocket the resignations of his cabinet colleagues. George V
received him with great kindness and sympathy. He both liked
and trusted his Prime Minister, and this feeling was most
cordially returned and was to have a decisive effect in the drama
which now followed. George V, having heard all about the
latest developments, suggested that a National government
should be formed, with MacDonald at its head, to cope with the
immediate emergency. The King stressed that there was no one

more likely to be able to lead the country out of its present troubles. MacDonald was both flattered and touched by this, and in the end he agreed.

The Labour Party never forgave him; every form of insult and invective was heaped on his head by men who had been his friends and colleagues for nearly forty years. They accused him (unjustly) of treachery, disloyalty, snobbery and deceit. Day after day, as Prime Minister in the National Government, he had to face, across the floor of the House of Commons, the cold, hostile expressions of men who had been his comrades in arms for half a lifetime.

They showed him no mercy; they did their best to make him miserable and they succeeded.

Chequers, to MacDonald as to Neville Chamberlain after him, was a veritable refuge, a source of solace and refreshment to which he could escape at weekends. But his delight in the place was used by his enemies in the Labour Party as a further stick with which to beat him. He was accused, as time went on, of neglecting public duties so that he might rush off early on Fridays to Chequers, where he delighted in "Lording it as a *grand seigneur*" over the weekend. Later on one extremely vituperative article written by Snowden in a Sunday newspaper contained an illustration of MacDonald lying full length on the grass near Chequers in an attitude and attire evidently intended to convey indolence and sloth. This so annoyed the King that he told his secretary to protest to Snowden, but he replied that he had only written the article and had not chosen and was not responsible for the illustration.

In 1932, for the first but not for the last time, a Prime Minister's daughter was married from Chequers. On 20th September the wedding took place at the Methodist chapel at Wendover of Sheila MacDonald, and there was a reception afterwards at Chequers, where there was a large marquee in the grounds.

Ramsay MacDonald was not, during his time at Chequers, a regular attender at the chapel at Wendover or at any place of worship. He preferred while he was there to spend his Sundays as far as possible in the open air. But this does not mean that he was not a religious man. When he was at Lossiemouth he never missed a Sunday going to church. Whether at Chequers, at Downing Street or in Lossiemouth, he always insisted on grace being said before meals. He was, in the words of his daughter, "a God-fearing man".

The advent of the National Government did not greatly affect the kind of people asked to Chequers at the weekends. MacDonald liked his guests to be people with whom he had some kind of affinity. They had to have some 'sparkle' in order to appeal to him. With the exception of Lord Thomson, and in an odd kind of way Thomas, this quality was conspicuous by its absence from his former Cabinet colleagues, of whom he had never had a very high opinion – a fact which he was at little pains to conceal. Nor did he find it among the members of the newly constituted government. He and Baldwin got on well enough together, but there was never any real affinity between them. Among his political associates during this sad part of his life the one from whose company he derived the most pleasure was probably Jowitt. He and his wife were always given a particularly warm welcome to Chequers, to which they were not infrequent visitors. Others to be invited during MacDonald's second Premiership included Bernard Shaw and Charles Chaplin, as well as certain members of the cast of the Oberammergau Passion Play, which MacDonald had been to more than once and had greatly enjoyed.

In June 1935 Baldwin succeeded Ramsay MacDonald and returned to Chequers. During the time since they had last been there both Baldwin and Mrs Baldwin had kept in touch with Lord and Lady Lee. At Christmas 1930, Mrs Baldwin had written:

Dear Lady Lee,
 I want to thank you myself for the Christmas card that you have sent us of your old home and the new. I don't know how to put it, but I do feel so sorry that you have thought it advisable to leave your lovely home for the second time – First beautiful Chequers that "house of Ancient Memories" which you both gave your full hearts to – a memento of all that is generous and noble for all time. Then having made a fresh lovely home that too – owing to your gift – has not been possible to keep. In our way . . . Stanley made a gift to the Nation – and now owing to the dearness and kindness of friends they have made it possible for us to live where we do in Eaton Square. – I know that you don't regret your gift, no more

than we do our less magnificent one and I personally would not have it otherwise. One just feels that it is one of the mysteries of God that having given with both hands in good times a time comes when it isn't possible any more to do anything but just manage. . . .

And in June 1931 Baldwin himself wrote to tell Lee that "You are in my category of those who think out with as much care what you can do to help with your money as most people take to invest it and many to dodge their taxes. I like to think that we are friends."

In the General Election which took place in November 1935 the Conservatives were returned with a comfortable majority. The year 1936 did not open well for Baldwin, however. There was a howl of rage when the terms of the Hoare Laval Pact became known. Baldwin was forced to jettison Hoare as Foreign Secretary in favour of Anthony Eden.

At the end of the first week in March 1936, Baldwin had gone as usual to Chequers for the weekend. On the morning of Saturday 7th March, he received a telephone call from Eden, who said he wanted to see him immediately on an urgent matter. Baldwin at once agreed and Eden set off for Chequers. The news which he brought was disturbing; it was that that very morning German troops, in breach not only of the Treaty of Versailles but also of that of Locarno, had entered the de-militarized Rhineland. Baldwin did not say much as Eden proceeded with his narrative but pulled away steadily at his pipe. He then said that, though he personally was friendly to the French, he was quite clear in his mind that there would be no support in Britain for any military action by them. With this, Eden "could only agree". Eden also told Baldwin that in view of Hitler's repeated assurance that he would respect the Treaty of Locarno (which had been freely negotiated by Germany), he did not feel that he was any longer to be trusted. Baldwin did not dissent from this and said that they must now await the French reaction to this latest move by Hitler.

Time passed; the days lengthened and the spring came. The month of May is perhaps the most beautiful of all at Chequers. One weekend towards the end of the month, Tom Jones, one of the Cabinet secretaries, was staying there. It was lovely weather, the spring greenery was at its freshest and its best, the horse chestnuts were in full bloom, and Stanley Baldwin was in expansive mood. The talk turned on Winston Churchill.

"One of these days I'll make a few casual remarks about Winston," he said. "Not a speech – no oratory – just a few words in passing. I've got it all ready. I am going to say that when Winston was born lots of fairies swooped down on his cradle with gifts – imagination, eloquence, industry, ability, and then came a fairy who said 'No one person has a right to so many gifts', picked him up and gave him such a shake and twist that with all these gifts he was denied judgement and wisdom. And that is why while we delight to listen to him in the House we do not take his advice."

Baldwin also said around this time, when asked why he had not brought Churchill into the government that it was "quite likely there would be a war" and, if so, Churchill would be "the obvious person to run it", and it would be much better for him then to go in with a completely free hand and not compromised in any way by having been a member of a pre-war government.

Those of Baldwin's guests who did not have cars of their own were invariably met by the Prime Minister's chauffeur at Wendover station, and when they arrived at Chequers, Baldwin would often be standing at the front door to greet them with Ethel in her chocolate-brown uniform beside him. Baldwin would at once offer his guest a drink, but this generally turned out not to be a cocktail or a whiskey and soda but a tumbler of Cuff's Malvern water. This was Baldwin's favourite drink, and he generally took it himself and offered it to his guests before retiring for the night.

The Baldwins were alone at Chequers the weekend when Jones stayed. When Baldwin learnt that his guest had had an extremely harassing day and had only had a sandwich lunch, he produced a bottle of champagne. After dinner, they went up to the Long Gallery. Baldwin paced up and down and recited part of a speech which he had recently made to the 1922 club, in the course of which he had argued that "we could not have got the country to re-arm one moment earlier than we did". Jones had recently returned from Germany, where he had seen Hitler and Ribbentrop. Baldwin, after explaining that "my wife and I are one" asked Jones to tell them about his visit. This Jones did, relating how when told that Baldwin was a "shy and modest statesman who had never got over his surprise at being Prime Minister", Hitler had remarked "And I also." Hitler had evinced a keen desire to meet Baldwin. But the Prime Minister had never flown, and disliked the sea, and he inquired whether Hitler would be willing to fly to England and land as near as possible to Chequers. Hitler never came to Chequers, but Ribbentrop went there in 1937.

During the weekend, Baldwin kept on referring to the question of his retirement. "I have made my contribution such as it was," he said. Then the conversation turned to religion, and Baldwin spoke "simply and intensely" of his belief that "God could still make some use of him." He said that, "As one grew old, one's prayers became shorter – just sighs and interjections." Shortly after this, the talk turned again to foreign affairs, and Baldwin said, "For three days I had terrible anxiety when Germany re-entered the demilitarized zone and there were people clamouring that we should reoccupy the Rhineland."

At this time of year Baldwin liked to take his guests round the Chequers garden, of which he was fond, but his thoughts kept turning to Astley Hall with the lilac, laburnums and hawthorn at their best. He had not been able to enjoy the spring blossoms at his Worcestershire home since the war, he would complain.

There is no doubt that, although he had only been Prime Minister for a year Baldwin was already feeling the strain. Any major effort and particularly the making of an important speech reduced him to a state of nervous exhaustion. He spent that Whitsuntide (1936) at Chequers, and immediately afterwards he cancelled all his engagements in order to enable him to stay on there for a further week. The staff looked after him extremely well, and there is no doubt that the rest did him a great deal of good.

As during the MacDonald so during the Baldwin period there is a remarkable absence from the visitors' book of the names of important members of the Cabinet. The fact is that, with one or two exceptions, Baldwin was never particularly close to his political associates. He had what has been described as "an almost reverential admiration" for Lord Halifax. In the House of Commons his greatest friend was J. C. C. Davidson. The Davidsons, who, incidentally had first met one another through the Baldwins, were his most frequent visitors at Chequers. With most of the members of his Cabinet he was never on intimate terms, and he seldom asked any of them to his weekend retreat.

"Some of my colleagues think that I am a half wit; others doubt whether I am a quarter wit," he is reported once to have said, "I can understand their opinion and their doubts but I cannot understand why those who doubt and those who disagree with me should still retain office in my cabinet. Edward Wood (Halifax) and William Bridgeman talk the same language I do; my other colleagues don't."

Whereas MacDonald's first visitor to Chequers had been Lord Londonderry, it had been Baldwin's great delight to welcome there important Trade Union leaders. One such was Walter Citrine, who drove down for lunch early in November 1936; he had recently returned from the United States.

After lunch Baldwin asked Citrine to follow him into his study and then invited him to sit down in an armchair. The Prime Minister himself paced restlessly backwards and forwards in front of the fire for several seconds. Then he suddenly came to a standstill and asked his guest abruptly whether he had heard anything about the King while he was in America. "Yes," came the reply.

"You know all about the King and Mrs Simpson then?"

"Yes," said Citrine. "The American newspapers are full of it and, indeed, I felt a sense of personal humiliation at the scurrilous allusions to the King's alleged carrying on with a married woman."

The Prime Minister then said that he had been to see the King and had addressed His Majesty as follows: "You may think me Victorian. You may think my views are out of date, but I believe I know how to interpret the minds of our own people and I say that people expect a higher standard from their King. People are talking about you and this American woman, Mrs Simpson. I have had many nasty letters written by people who respected your father but who don't like the way you are going on. . . . I don't believe you can go on like this and get away with it."

After repeating these remarks, Baldwin paused and then said, "You know Citrine, I like him and I felt sorry for him when he said pathetically to me 'I know there is nothing kingly about me, but I have tried to mix with the people and make them think I was one of them.' " After a further pause, the Prime Minister continued, "I told him pretty straight that I expected the divorce would go through, but what then? What about six months after? What would happen then? I again told him that I did not want a reply from him then but I have heard something since which makes me think that although I expected my conversation to have straightened him up a bit he may do something foolish."

Citrine asked him what he meant and Baldwin said, "Well, he might marry her before the coronation and think he can get away with it. On the other hand he might abdicate and marry her. He is fascinated by her and it is a difficult job to break him away." After an interval, the Prime Minister said that he had consulted Attlee (recently elected leader of the Labour Party) and then asked Citrine his opinion as to the attitude he (Baldwin) had taken. Citrine assured him that he was undoubtedly interpreting the minds of the people in the Labour movement. Baldwin promised to keep him informed.

Amongst the King's and Mrs Simpson's circle of friends was a certain Mrs Herman Rogers, who was Lady Lee's cousin. Before her marriage, she had been Miss Katherine Moore, and she and her sister were the co-heiresses of the Moore trust estate. Mr and Mrs Rogers, as well as Mrs Simpson, were amongst the King's guests on board the *Nahlin* during the Adriatic cruise which caused such widespread comment. When, shortly before the abdication, Mrs Simpson felt compelled to leave England, it was to the Rogers' villa in the south of France that she went.

Baldwin's handling of the Abdication crisis considerably enhanced his prestige, which had fallen disastrously as a result of the Hoare Laval Pact. His reputation was as high and the strength of party allegiance to him as strong as either had ever been when, at the end of May 1937, he resigned and Neville Chamberlain succeeded him as Prime Minister. In the course of his last evening in the House of Commons, Baldwin told Robert

Boothby that his great regret was that he had not taken more interest in foreign affairs.

Before leaving Chequers for the last time, Mrs Baldwin wrote to Lady Lee to thank her and Lord Lee "for all that it has been to us on and off for over $14\frac{1}{2}$ years".

9

A Prime Minister who
Loved Chequers

OF all the Prime Ministers who have occupied Chequers, Neville Chamberlain was probably the one that was fondest of it. Perhaps this was partly because, unlike most of the others, his roots lay not in the countryside but in the city of Birmingham, and Chequers was therefore something quite new to him. From the moment that he first set foot in it he liked everything about it – the house, the furniture, the pictures, the garden and, above all, the park and the trees. Like Ramsay MacDonald he was never happier than when, with axe or spade in hand, he was working away among the woodlands, and he personally bound up one of the old trees which was in danger of falling down. He had always been a keen naturalist, and while he was at Chequers he managed to make a close study of the trees and wrote a monograph on them which Eden, who discovered it later, described as "charming and erudite". Little more than a fortnight after he had become Prime Minister, he wrote to Lee, expressing great appreciation of the place and telling him:

We have already explored the box woods, visited Cymbeline's castle, searched (vainly) for the Druid's Maze, discovered new flowers and ascended Beacon and Coombe Hills. We have also made a tour of the house and started a preliminary examination of its pictures and other treasures. The rest must wait until we come back and I hope that won't be long.

What trees there are here! I have never seen such magnificent specimens as the Yew, the tulip tree, the horse chestnut, not to speak of the oaks, beeches, limes and elms. . . .

And ten days later Mrs Chamberlain wrote to Lady Lee telling her:

I was thrilled to find the fort of Cymbeline all ready for me so close to the house. It would have amused you could you have seen us on the downs that first morning. We were both so excited and thrilled with everything – Neville with moths, butterflies, flowers and birds, and I by the thought of Cymbeline's abode. After we had been going on for some time, Neville suddenly turned to me and said "Do you realise that we have both been talking hard for the last ten minutes and neither has been listening to a word the other has said!"

Neville Chamberlain possessed in a quite remarkable degree the seeing eye for birds and flowers and trees and all the beautiful things of nature and the ability to cast all other thoughts from his mind at will on a country walk or when he was engaged in some favourite pastime. These qualities were at the same time fortified and given full scope by Chequers.

It is interesting to notice that Chamberlain was the first Prime Minister to spend Christmas at Chequers. Indeed he went there for each of the three Christmases during which he held that office.

The Chamberlains were a most united and devoted family and it is not surprising, therefore, to find that not only Chamberlain's son and daughter but also other members of his family were frequently visitors to Chequers. Prominent among these latter were his two sisters, Hilda and Ida, his companions and confidantes from childhood onwards, to whom he had written a regularly weekly letter for more than twenty years. They lived at Odiham in Hampshire and took great pride and pleasure in their garden, and it afforded him considerable pleasure to show them round Chequers – the house and the garden and, above all, his beloved park and trees and to tell them about his ideas for them.

In the third week of October 1937 the Lees went to stay at Chequers as the guests of the Chamberlains. This was the first time that Lord and Lady Lee had been back there since the place had ceased to be their property. When they arrived they found their former butler, who had seen them off when they left in January 1921, at the door to greet them. In spite of the fact that Chamberlain himself was laid up with gout the whole of the time they were there, the visit was a great success. The keen interest in and appreciation of the place and its history which the Chamberlains so clearly displayed was bound to be of particular satisfaction to its former owners. Their fellow guests were Lord and Lady Hailsham and the Maurice Hankeys. The Lees went to stay there again the following May, the party on that occasion including the Joe Kennedys (the American ambassador) and his wife, the Oliver Stanleys and David Margesson.

On Sunday morning, 16th January 1938, Chequers was the scene of an important meeting between Chamberlain and Anthony Eden, the Foreign Secretary, who was just back from a short holiday in the south of France. On 13th January, while he was away, there had arrived a cable addressed to the Foreign Office by the British Embassy in Washington. It contained Roosevelt's suggestion that he should summon the entire Diplomatic Corps to a meeting at the White House and address them on international affairs with a view to reducing tension and working out proposals for enhancing the prospects of world peace. Eden being away, the Foreign Office immediately sent the papers to the Prime Minister, who was at Chequers at that time. Chamberlain, who was about to enter with Mussolini on negotiations of which he had great hopes, while thanking the President, replied, politely and immediately, that he did not think the moment was ripe for the conference which Roosevelt contemplated.

Eden got back to London on the evening of 16th January. The next day (Sunday) he travelled down to Chequers to have lunch with the Prime Minister. When he arrived, he found Chamberlain in excellent humour, though he himself was not. He was, in fact, extremely annoyed with Chamberlain, firstly for 'pouring cold water' on Roosevelt's plan and secondly and still more so because he felt he ought to have been consulted by Chamberlain before the reply was sent to Washington. The Prime Minister's answer to this was that he was anxious to get the talks started with Mussolini as soon as possible, and there had not been time to consult Eden, who was out of the country at the time.

Before having lunch, the Prime Minister and the Foreign Secretary went out for a walk together, and it was apparent that by then a certain stiffness had developed between them. Eden had written to the British Ambassador in Washington the evening before without consulting Chamberlain, who evidently resented this and refused to endorse the message. The Prime Minister seemed to believe in the possibility of a 'genuine settlement' with the dictators, and when Eden expostulated with him he was told that the Foreign Office was "not sincere in its efforts". The discussion was continued after lunch and seems to have become increasingly acrimonious as Eden expatiated on and Chamberlain belittled the value of Roosevelt's initiative. They talked also about the Italian 'volunteers' in Spain, and Eden said that he had "no more confidence in Mussolini's promises". Chamberlain, on the other hand, thought that we had "a wonderful chance of coming to terms with Italy about the future of the Mediterranean". The rift between the two men continued to widen during the ensuing weeks until towards the end of February Eden resigned.

Rather over seven months later, on a fine Saturday afternoon in the early autumn of 1938, Neville Chamberlain was to be seen walking past Crow's Close and making his way along the path which leads to Ellesborough Church. This was one of his favourite walks, and there were few nicer times of year at which to take it. But this was just after he had returned from Munich, and now, as he walked along past the great beech trees, the appalling strain of the last few days was clearly telling on him. "We came here immediately after lunch," he wrote to his sisters, "and walked up through Crows' Close to the Chequers church way. I came nearer to a nervous breakdown then than I have ever come in my life. I have pulled myself together for there is a fresh ordeal to go through in the House."

Lee had been a firm supporter of Neville Chamberlain over Munich, and as a token of his admiration for him he decided to present to Chequers a large and beautiful service of silver-gilt plate inscribed "In grateful homage to Neville Chamberlain." The Prime Minister, in thanking him, wrote:

My dear Arthur,
    My wife told me of your noble gift last week, but I preferred to wait until I could see it myself before writing to thank you for it. When I got down on Friday it was all set out for me in the

dining room and my breath was quite taken away by its splendour. I hardly knew which to admire most, the simplicity of the plates and knives and forks, or the imposing decoration of the bowls, or the elegance and craftsmanship of the candelabra. I shall certainly never be content to reserve it for foreigners; it will come out whenever I have guests here and I and all my successors will be proud to show it on our table.

In inscribing it to me you have done me great and lasting honour, which I value all the more because I am so devoted to Chequers and get such infinite pleasure out of the use of it that I do want my memory to be somehow associated with it after I have gone. So you have done something which is specially gratifying to me. And you have added greatly to it by the terms of your letter, which will find its place among my archives. . . .

For a short time it had seemed to Neville Chamberlain that his hope of "Peace for our time" might be satisfied, but this hope received a cruel blow when Hitler marched into Prague in March 1939, and it was finally smashed by the German invasion of Poland the following September. "Everything that I have worked for, everything that I have hoped for, everything that I have believed in during my public life has crashed into ruins," he said.

Then, early in May 1940, came the debate on the Norwegian campaign; and it was as a result of this that he became convinced of the necessity of a coalition government. When he discovered that the Labour leaders were unwilling to serve under him he went at once to Buckingham Palace and tendered his resignation. Later the same day the King sent for Winston Churchill, who kissed hands on his appointment as Prime Minister.

The next day, Chamberlain wrote to his sisters and told them (amongst other things) that:

Winston doesn't want us to move from this house [10 Downing Street] for a month or even longer and then (if the Government still stands) we are to go back to No. 11. But Chequers! I shall have to go there some time to collect my things and say goodbye. It will be a hard wrench to part with that place where I have been so happy.

The following weekend Chamberlain went down to Chequers to say goodbye. This was indeed for him a very sad parting. He wrote to his sisters that he had remained there "just long enough

to say goodbye to the staff . . . and to look round my trees and
the gardens. I am content now I have done that and shall put
Chequers out of my mind. We have had some happy days there,
but they are over anyhow and it is difficult to see how there can
be much more happiness for any of us."

Neville Chamberlain's premiership marked the end of what
might be called "the old order" at Chequers – as of so many
other things in England. The place was still run on very much
the same lines as in the time of the Lees, with several of the
original staff (including Ethel) still there. But the shoe was
already starting to pinch financially, and the time was fast
approaching when the endowment provided by Lee, generous
though it was, would prove insufficient. Partly this was due to
the way in which the place was run. Coming there one winter
weekend, Chamberlain's daughter counted nineteen fires lit in
the different rooms (including bedrooms) and found that baths
were run before dinner whether the visitors wanted them or not.
Since the defalcations previously referred to, a new system of
managing the housekeeping money had been introduced. The
dismissed housekeeper had been succeeded by Mrs Sinclair and
she in turn by Miss Lamont, who was now the curator, and she
and Mrs Chamberlain got on splendidly. The Prime Minister's
wife had no housekeeping worries at all. She did not even have to
order the meals unless there was something that she particularly
wanted, and there very seldom was. All the Chamberlains had
to do was to say how many people would be coming for the
weekend, and everything else was arranged for them. This was
entirely to their liking.

On 23rd June 1940 Chamberlain wrote his final letter of
thanks for his times at Chequers to Lee.

10

The Greatest of Them All

WINSTON CHURCHILL arrived at Chequers on 1st June 1940, his guests for this weekend being Brendan Bracken and Lord Beaverbrook. It was twenty years since his last and only previous visit when he had gone there at the invitation of Lloyd George to attend the conference of senior Cabinet Ministers on the future of the coalition. Most of the intervening years had been spent by him in the political wilderness.

Churchill had never been popular with the bulk of the Conservative Party, and it had come as a great surprise to most of them and a source of annoyance to many when, in 1924, on the formation of his second government, Baldwin had invited him to become Chancellor of the Exchequer. After the 1929 General Election, however, a rift started to develop between the two men, the chief cause of which was that Churchill disagreed with Baldwin's policy on India. The rift widened after the formation of the National Government, when Churchill became increasingly critical of Baldwin on the issue of Defence. Churchill's criticisms were resented not so much by Baldwin himself as by his supporters. One prominent Conservative described Churchill around this time as "a dog biting the hand that had fed him". To this Churchill replied that he hoped that what was meant was that he was the kind of faithful old watchdog which, when it finds his master asleep and a burglar at hand about to steal his possessions, gives him a gentle little nip on the hand to wake him up. Then he added, "But while we're on this subject of dogs, there's another kind of dog – the nasty mangy dog that fawns upon the hand it hopes will feed him. Now I don't want to be unkind about this particular dog because it's really quite a nice little dog and it's obviously very, very hungry."

All this did not tend to diminish Churchill's unpopularity

with the Conservatives or to lessen the feeling among the place hunters and seekers after directorships and judgeships on the Conservative benches that he was a man to associate with whom was dangerous, a man to be avoided at all costs.

The *nadir* of Churchill's political fortunes had come in December 1936, when he addressed the House of Commons on the constitutional issue raised by Edward VIII's desire to marry Mrs Simpson. When he pleaded for delay and careful delibera- tion and asked that no "irrevocable step" should be taken for the time being he was greeted with loud cries of "Sit down," and at one time he was unable to make himself heard. Though the noise was mainly made by the Conservatives, opposition to Churchill on this issue was by no means confined to them, for, in his handling of the abdication question, public opinion was solidly behind Baldwin.

Ever since Hitler had seized power in Germany in January 1933, Churchill had been among the few British politicians to appreciate the danger of a resurgent Germany, and in the ensuing years, he had warned the Government, the House of Commons and the nation about the Nazi menace, had drawn attention to the deficiencies in our defences and had pleaded for more active rearmament. Both his warnings and his pleas had gone largely unheeded. In March 1938, he said in the House of Commons:

> For five years I have talked to the House on these matters not with great success. I have watched this famous island descending incontinently, fecklessly the stairway which leads to a dark gulf. It is a fine broad stairway at the beginning but after a bit the carpet ends. A little further on there are only flagstones and a little further on still these break beneath your feet. Look back over the last five years since, that is to say, Germany began to re-arm in earnest and openly to seek revenge. . . . If mortal catastrophe should overtake the British nation and the British Empire, his- torians a thousand years hence will still be baffled by the mystery of our affairs. They will never understand how it was that a victorious nation, with everything in hand, suffered themselves to be brought low and to cast away all that they had gained by measureless sacrifice and absolute victory – gone with the wind.

The arrival of Churchill constitutes an important watershed in the history of Chequers for two reasons. The first is that he was incomparably the greatest man ever to occupy it. The second is the difference that it made in the way the place was run. From the beginning of the Second World War onwards all the domestic work was done by a detachment of the women's military services – W.R.N.S., A.T.S. or W.A.A.F.s under the control of the curator, Miss Lamont. But Mrs Churchill, without in any way supplanting the authority of Miss Lamont, managed most successfully to make Chequers the country home of the Churchill family for the duration of the war, Chartwell being closed for virtually the whole of this period. At different stages of the war, Mrs Churchill was there quite a lot while the Prime Minister was away. She has probably spent more time there than any other Prime Minister's wife, and her influence on the place, both inside and out, always most tactfully exercised, has been very great.

It is unquestionable that Chequers never rivalled Chartwell in Churchill's affections. From his point of view, it had the drawback that he could not stamp his own personality on it – unlike Chartwell where he could constantly be devising fresh projects. But he enormously appreciated Chequers and fully recognized it as the great boon that it undoubtedly was in providing him with a place where he could get a complete change of atmosphere at weekends. He himself said, at a trustees' meeting in June 1941, that during the previous twelve months he had used it more than any of the previous Prime Ministers had done in a similar period, and he did not know how he could have carried on the government of the country without it. Chequers alone, he declared, had made it possible to keep work going over the weekend, and to get to know the generals, admirals and air marshals whom he had appointed or was thinking of appointing. To choose one of them merely as a result of a staff or cabinet meeting or a visit to one of their headquarters was rather like "buying a pig in a poke", he added.

There were many family reunions at Chequers during the Churchill epoch, and one of the happiest occurred at the christening of the Prime Minister's grandson. The visitors' book contains the following entry: "October 10th 1940 4.40 a.m. – Winston". This was a unique event – the birth of Churchill's first grandson, the only time any of the Prime Ministers has had a descendant born at Chequers, indeed the first time for more than a hundred years that a birth had occurred in the old house. The christening itself was at Ellesborough church rather over six weeks later, namely on Sunday 1st December. This was the only occasion on which Churchill himself went to church during the whole of the time he was at Chequers, though Mrs Churchill and other members of the family went there quite frequently. The Prime Minister gave a lunch party afterwards, to which the Rector was invited. When someone rose to propose the baby's health, Churchill got up and interrupted, saying: "As it was *my* birthday yesterday, I am going to ask you all to drink *my* health first." There was an immediate storm of protest with cries of, "Sit down Daddy", but at first he refused to give way. Ultimately, however, he was made to resume his seat and Winston junior was duly toasted, and then Lord Beaverbrook got up and proposed the health of Winston senior, whom he described as "the greatest man in the world", wishing him every success and promising him all possible help in the production of Spitfires.

No other Prime Minister has been more generous in his expenditure on Chequers. The avenue of beech trees cost him more than £300. And, though during the war itself there was the handicap of rationing as well as other restrictions, none of the others has ever spent the amount on entertainment that he did during the time that he was Prime Minister. A rule was established under which the Prime Minister was allowed to draw fifteen pounds from the funds to cover the cost of expenses for each period of not less than thirty-six hours spent at Chequers during any seven consecutive days. Anything additional to this had to come out of his own resources. Most of the Prime Ministers have kept within this limit, but Churchill made no attempt to do so. He once described it as just about sufficient to provide food and drink for the chauffeurs who brought his guests down for the weekend.

During the war Churchill spent almost every weekend at Chequers, except when he was out of the country or when there was a full moon, at which latter time it was considered dangerous for him to go there because the long straight drive, with the river running alongside, made it too easy a target for enemy bombers. On these occasions he went instead to Ditchley Park, the Oxfordshire home of Mr and Mrs Ronald Tree.

A regular routine soon established itself for the Chequers weekends. Some time on Friday afternoon or evening the cavalcade would leave Downing Street. Three large, black Daimlers drew up outside the garden entrance. Usually there was a long wait before the great man was ready – then a scurry for writing pads, notebooks and boxes, and then secretaries, typists, and detectives piled into the three cars. Last of all came the Prime Minister himself, who was handed overcoat, gloves and stick by the valet and then took the seat behind the driver in the leading motor car. A typist nearly always sat next to him. He never wasted a second if he could possibly avoid it. Often he would dictate letters, speeches or minutes the whole way from Downing Street to Chequers, only stopping now and then to urge the chauffeur to drive faster.

What happened at Chequers when they got there depended on the time of arrival. If it was fairly early Churchill would go to bed for an hour or so before having his bath. Dinner was never before eight-thirty and sometimes not till much later. If, as was generally the case, the guests included high-ranking serving officers or members of the Government the conversation during this as during all other meals at which they were present was almost always entirely about the war, a subject which Churchill's mind hardly ever left until hostilities ceased. He did not believe in wasting a single second. He frequently but not invariably came down to dinner attired in a boiler suit and flowered silk dressing gown, and when the meal was over there was almost always a film show in the long gallery when such old favourites as *Lady Hamilton* were played again and again. There were those who complained about the long conferences going on into the small hours of the morning when tired generals, admirals or air marshals were longing to get to bed. A vivid picture has been given by Lord Alanbrooke of one such evening:

> Finally at 2.15 a.m. he suggested we should proceed to the hall to have some sandwiches, and I hoped this might at last mean bed. But, no! We went on till ten to three before he made a move for bed. He had the gramophone turned on, and, in the many-coloured dressing-gown, with a sandwich in one hand and water-cress in the other, he trotted round and round the hall, giving occasional little skips to the tune of the gramophone. On each lap

near the fireplace, he stopped to release some priceless quotation or thought. For instance he quoted a saying that a man's life is similar to a walk down a long passage with closed windows on either side. As you reach each window, an unknown hand opens it and the light it lets in only increases by contrast the darkness of the end of the passage.

Once Churchill had retired for the night, nothing and nobody was normally allowed to disturb him. But as soon as he woke up he rang the bell, and then his breakfast would be brought to him, together with his 'box', into which one of his secretaries had placed the numerous papers with which he had to deal – his correspondence, foreign office and military telegrams and the minutes and other communications made to him by members of the Government, the chiefs of staff and others. A typist would also come in to find out if there was anything he wished to dictate. He generally remained in bed, working steadily at his papers, for most of the morning. From time to time one of his secretaries would come in bringing any new papers which had arrived and collecting those which had been dealt with. These latter were normally sent by dispatch rider to London, except in cases of extreme urgency marked by the Prime Minister "Action this day", when the message would be sent through on the 'scrambler' telephone. A number of his special red "Action this day" labels had always to be available at his bedside.

The time at which Churchill got up depended on a number of factors, including the weather and the time of year. On a fine day in summer, he might have his 'box' taken down into the garden and continue working on his papers there. Again, if important visitors were at Chequers he might decide on a formal discussion with them at about noon. This would last for about an hour and would take place either in his study or the Hawtrey Room. At other times he and Mrs Churchill would meet their guests for drinks before lunch in the White Parlour. At some time in the afternoon or early evening Churchill invariably went to bed and to sleep. There was no set time for this siesta. It would depend on who was at Chequers at the time and what was happening, but it always lasted for at least an hour.

There were certain people who went regularly to Chequers whenever the Prime Minister was there. General Sir Hastings

Ismay ('Pug') was one of these. He acted as the link between Churchill and the military machine. He provided, in his own words, "a two-way channel of communication", finding out from the service chiefs and others in Whitehall the things which Churchill wanted to know and also communicating to them the Prime Minister's views and wishes in regard to the conduct of the war. In enabling him to fulfil this difficult task, Chequers played its part. Sometimes, when Churchill was contemplating appointing some officer to an important post, Ismay would take the individual in question out for a walk and deftly find out the things that the Prime Minister wanted to know about him, while Churchill himself remained in bed. Or another Chequers walk might be devoted to telling a general just given an important new command something about the Prime Minister and giving the general a few hints about how to get on with him.

Ismay himself was adept at getting on well with Churchill, and during the Chequers weekends he knew just when to be at hand and when to keep out of the way. After dinner, when the film show was over, if there was no important officer or Minister to whom he wanted to talk, Churchill would sometimes wander from room to room until he found the place that suited him best to work. If he saw he was by himself, Ismay would go and sit with him and remain there in silence just in case he was wanted. One night in October 1940 Ismay and Churchill were alone in the Hawtrey Room. The Prime Minister looked tired out, and Ismay thought there was a chance of getting to bed in reasonable time. But suddenly Churchill jumped up and exclaimed "I believe I can do it." Bells were rung, secretaries and typists appeared and Churchill started to dictate his broadcast to the French people and continued to do so well into the small hours of the morning.

Professor Lindemann ('The Prof') also came practically every weekend. He was a strict vegetarian for whom special meals had to be prepared. A room was always kept available for him, but he never stayed the night at Chequers if he could avoid it. However late he was kept up by Churchill he almost invariably returned to his own quarters at Oxford to sleep, as he preferred his own bed. He was Churchill's chief adviser on scientific matters, and he had immense power and influence in consequence. The Prime Minister had the greatest admiration for what he described as Lindemann's "beautiful brain". He (Lindemann) brought with him to Chequers vital statistics, illustrated by graphs and many coloured charts which gave Churchill exactly the information he needed about U-boat sinkings, aircraft production, food and coal stocks and innumerable other subjects.

Early in January 1941 there arrived at Chequers one of the most important and at the same time one of the strangest visitors ever to go there. He was almost incredibly untidy, pale-faced and seedy looking. His clothes looked, it has been said, as though he made a habit of sleeping in them and his hat as though he made a habit of sitting on it. The apparel proclaimed the man. He had no money and, in his own right, no position. But, coming as he did at one of the darkest moments in British history, his visit was of enormous importance. For with him, when he arrived from America, he had brought a letter addressed to the King of England. It was as follows:

Your Majesty,

I have designated the Honourable Harry L. Hopkins as my personal representative on a special mission to Great Britain. Mr. Hopkins is a very good friend of mine in whom I repose the utmost confidence.

I am asking him to convey to you and Her Majesty the Queen my cordial greetings and my sincere hope that his mission may advance the common ideals of our two nations.

Cordially your friend
Franklin D. Roosevelt

Hopkins, the son of a small storekeeper and harness maker in Sioux City, Iowa, had always been very keen on social work and had been appointed during the time that Roosevelt was Governor of New York to be Deputy Chairman of the Relief Organization, a body set up to cope with the effects of the Depression in that State. The zeal which he displayed soon attracted Roosevelt's attention. But there was more to it than that. Hopkins, poor and an invalid, aroused Roosevelt's sympathy and protectiveness from the beginning of their strange and fateful association. Hopkins worshipped Roosevelt and served him with unstinted devotion, and there was no sacrifice that he would not gladly have made for his chief. "I can understand that you wonder why I need that half man around," the President once said to Wendell Wilkie, referring to Hopkins. "But some day you may well be sitting here where I am now as President of the United States. And when you are you'll be looking at that door over there and knowing that practically everyone that walks through it wants something out of you. You'll learn, what a lonely job this is, and you'll discover the need for somebody like Harry Hopkins, who asks for nothing except to serve you."

Hopkins' devotion to his chief was proverbial and sometimes a little embarrassing even to Roosevelt. There was one occasion when a very important government official was trying to get the President to alter one of his decisions. Hopkins was sent over to try to win over the official in question to Roosevelt's point of view. After they had had a few preliminary skirmishes, Hopkins suddenly turned to the man he was supposed to be pacifying and said, "Why, you presumptuous louse, how can you have the nerve to try to get the greatest man in the world to change his mind after he's made it up?"

In his journey to England, Hopkins had flown to Lisbon in an American aircraft, but the last part of his travelling was done in a B.O.A.C. clipper, in which he landed at Poole in Dorset. Brendan Bracken, a member of the Government, had travelled down specially to Poole to meet him on Churchill's instructions, but so sick was Hopkins that he was unable to unfasten his safety belt and disembark with the rest of the passengers. So Bracken was forced to go on board, and it was quite a long time before Hopkins felt well enough to get out. Churchill had given instructions that everything possible was to be done to provide for the comfort of this important visitor. The most modern of Pullman cars was attached to the train, the conductors wore white gloves and an excellent meal was provided, with wines and liqueurs, and newspapers and periodicals of every kind were there for him to read if he wanted to. As the train reached Clapham Junction the air raid sirens went, and within a few minutes of its arrival at Waterloo incendiaries were being showered down on the piece of line along which they had just passed. Hopkins had a narrow escape.

In the course of this visit, Hopkins went to Chequers three

Ramsay Macdonald and his daughter at Chequers in 1924: (*above*) in the South Garden, (*below*) in the Hawtrey Room

Stanley Baldwin in the South Garden in 1924

The meet of the Old Berkeley Hunt in 1926

times, spending the weekend there on each occasion. It has been said that he hated the place. Indeed one of his compatriots, a high-ranking serving officer, once remarked that, "Harry hates Chequers more than the Devil hates holy water." This was an exaggeration. In one of his letters, Hopkins referred to it as "this lovely old place". But he undoubtedly found it uncomfortable. With his wretched health, he felt the cold intensely, and Chequers in winter was never really warm. One of the reasons for this was the way it had been built with a large open courtyard in the middle, which Lee had had roofed in to make the great hall. There was no proper central heating, though Lee had put in one or two ineffective cylinders. Hopkins found that the only place in which he could avoid shivering was the downstairs bathroom, and to this sanctuary he repaired as often as he could to study his papers, clad in a large overcoat. He once told Mrs Churchill that if he could raise enough money after the war he would have proper central heating installed at Chequers.

In between his visits to Chequers Hopkins travelled widely all over England, interviewing every sort and kind of person, from Cabinet Ministers downwards, and examining for himself every aspect of the war effort. He also accompanied Churchill to Scotland. Halifax had just been appointed British ambassador to the United States; he was to fly to Washington and they had gone to see him off. On their return journey they stopped the night in Glasgow, where they attended a small, unofficial dinner given by the Lord Provost, at which Tom Johnston, Secretary of State for Scotland, was also present. Churchill and Johnston both made speeches and then Hopkins was asked to say a few words. He spoke quite simply and briefly of how much he had been impressed by all he had seen and heard in Britain. Then, towards the end of his remarks, he said, "I suppose you want to know what I shall say when I get back and see President Roosevelt. Well, I'm going to quote you one word from the Book of Books in the truth of which Mr Johnston's mother and my own Scotch mother were brought up: 'Whither thou goest, I will go, and where thou lodgest, I will lodge, thy people shall be my people and thy God my God.' " Then he added, speaking softly and with great intensity and looking hard at Churchill, "To the end". Nothing that Hopkins said while he was in

H

England impressed Churchill more than this. He knew full well what it meant.

The last of the three visits to Chequers which Hopkins made in the course of this particular tour took place on 8th February 1941, when he went there to say goodbye to Churchill. Churchill had invited him to spend the whole of the previous weekend with him at Chequers, but Hopkins knew that for most of it Wendell Wilkie, Roosevelt's opponent in the recent Presidential election, would be there, and he felt (rightly) that Wilkie would rather have Churchill to himself. So, instead, he had spent that weekend with Lord Beaverbrook at Cherkley. Now he found Churchill busily engaged in preparing an address to be broadcast to the nation, in which he would reply to a special message which Wilkie had brought over from Roosevelt, and he consulted Hopkins about various passages in it, particularly those which related to Lend Lease. After leaving Chequers, Hopkins, accompanied by Brendan Bracken, Commander Thompson and Lieutenant McComas, travelled by special train to Bournemouth. Lieutenant McComas flew back with him to Washington.

The speech about which the Prime Minister had consulted Hopkins was broadcast from the Hawtrey Room at Chequers immediately after the nine o'clock news on the evening of Sunday 9th February 1941. It was the first of Churchill's wartime addresses to be made from Chequers. He concluded with these words:

> The other day, President Roosevelt gave his opponent in the late Presidential Election a letter of introduction to me, and in it he wrote out a verse, in his own handwriting, from Longfellow, which he said "applies to you people as it does to us". Here is the verse:
>
> > . . . Sail on, O Ship of State!
> > Sail on, O Union, strong and great!
> > Humanity with all its fears,
> > With all the hopes of future years,
> > Is hanging breathless on thy fate!

What is the answer that I shall give, in your name, to this great man, the thrice-chosen head of a nation of one hundred and thirty millions? Here is the answer which I will give to President Roosevelt: Put your confidence in us. Give us your faith and your

blessing, and, under Providence, all will be well. We shall not fail
or falter; we shall not weaken or tire. Neither the sudden shock of
battle, nor the long-drawn trials of vigilance and exertion will
wear us down. Give us the tools and we will finish the job.

By the time that Churchill had been Prime Minister for
twelve months the security arrangements and the system of
communications which were to persist throughout the war had
been well established at Chequers. A watchman was always on
duty on the roof and a company of the Coldstream Guards was
stationed at Chequers, being housed in Nissen huts along the
side of the avenue adjoining the north park. Any of the officers
who wanted to were always allowed to join the party in the Long
Gallery for the evening film show. During the war, the army
took the defence of Chequers generally and the Prime Minister
in particular most seriously, a detailed plan having been worked
out which included calling for help from nearby units if needed.

Through lines were soon established to the Cabinet war room,
to the Whitehall 'annexe' and to the duty captain at the
Admiralty, so that news of a vital nature could be flashed
through immediately. A barbed-wire fence had been put up
round the gardens, sentries were on duty at every entrance
point, and detectives prowled about beating out the under-
growth and on the look-out for hiding places and vantage points
for spies and parachutists. In the grounds an outdoor range was
soon improvised where Churchill could practise shooting and
fire off a hundred rounds or so with his Wanliker rifle and then
an equal number from his Colt ·45 or his ·32 Webley Scott. He
was extremely proficient with all three. Here too he would,
now and again, fire off a few rounds with the Bren gun which he
caused to be carried about in his car, or he would attend
demonstrations of some piece of military equipment such as the
'bombard mortar' in which he was interested. Many strange
mechanisms were demonstrated in the park at Chequers during
those months.

The installation of the through line to the Duty Captain at the
Admiralty had been one of the first things that Churchill had
insisted on when he took over possession of Chequers. Similar
lines to the War Office and the Air Ministry soon followed, and
Churchill's last action before retiring to bed in the small hours

of the morning was often to seize each telephone in turn and ring up for the latest news. In the early months of 1941, now that the Battle of Britain had been won, it was the Battle of the Atlantic which dominated his thoughts. A twenty-four-hour watch was maintained at Chequers during the weekends, and there was someone always available to take urgent messages which might come through.

Normally Churchill never took any exercise unless it was absolutely essential that he should do so. He did not, as other Prime Ministers have, go for long walks through the country round Chequers for pleasure or the good of his health. But rifle and revolver practice were another matter. He would some-times climb the hills round about to carry out these exercises and to prepare for the attack by parachutists which he always envisaged as a possibility.

On Friday evening 23rd May 1941, Churchill had arrived as usual at Chequers, where his guests for the weekend were to include Averell Harriman and Generals Ismay and Pownall. The Battle of Crete was then at its height, and news had just come through that the German battleship *Bismarck* had put to sea, so everything pointed to an anxious weekend. As usual, Churchill kept his guests up until very late that evening and it was nearly three o'clock when he went to bed. Telephone messages had been reaching Chequers from the Admiralty all through the night, and in the small hours of the Saturday morn-ing (after Churchill had retired) the news came through that the *Hood* had been blown up. The rest of the weekend was taken up with anxieties about the whereabouts of the *Bismarck* and the plans for its destruction.

As the spring of 1941 turned to summer information started to reach the Foreign Office, and this caused Churchill's thoughts to be diverted from what was happening at sea to what was about to happen on land. Intelligence reports made it fairly clear that an attack by Hitler on Russia was imminent.

It was lovely weather when Churchill arrived at Chequers on the evening of Friday 20th June 1941. The Foreign Secretary, Anthony Eden, had been asked to come down on the Saturday and to spend the weekend. Others to be invited included Cranbourne, Beaverbrook, Cripps (British Ambassador to

Russia) and Winant. The American Ambassador had been the first to arrive. He had only just returned from the United States, having landed at Prestwick in the small hours of that same morning (Friday). A special aircraft had been sent to meet him and fly him south and he had completed the last part of his journey to Chequers by car, arriving in time for lunch. The others did not get there until considerably later in the day.

That night and the following day, Winant told Churchill of the conversations he had had with Roosevelt in Washington, when the President had promised extended patrols in the Atlantic, occupation of Iceland and a supporting statement to that of the British in the event of an attack by Hitler on Russia. It was this latter which loomed largest in the conversations at Chequers that weekend. Even before leaving the United States, Winant had learnt from intelligence reports of the possibility of such an attack. He discussed these reports both with his host and with others in the party. Cripps thought such an attack unlikely, but Churchill disagreed.

During dinner on the Friday evening the Prime Minister re-iterated that he regarded war between Russia and Germany as certain, and he spoke emphatically of the support which he intended to give to Stalin. When the meal was over Churchill went outside and strolled up and down the lawn, smoking one of his enormous cigars and talking to one of his secretaries, John Colville. In the course of their conversation, Colville asked him whether, as such an arch anti-communist, he was not being a little inconsistent in evincing such determination to support Stalin. "Not at all," he replied. "I have only one purpose and that is the destruction of Hitler, and my life is much simplified thereby. If Hitler invaded Hell, I would make at least a favourable reference to the Devil in the House of Commons."

At 4 a.m. the following morning news was received at Chequers that the German invasion of Russia had begun. Churchill had given orders that he was only to be woken up during the night in the event of the invasion of the United Kingdom. Accordingly, the latest news was not taken to his bedroom until 8 a.m. "Tell the B.B.C. I will broadcast at 9 p.m. tonight," he said. Then he told his valet to ask Eden to come and see him, at the same time sending the Foreign Secretary a

present of an enormous cigar on a silver salver. Eden at once
made his way to the Prime Minister's bedroom, and the two
statesmen had a short talk about this tremendous development.
Eden said he thought he ought to go at once to London and see
Maisky, the Russian ambassador, but he promised that he would
come back to Chequers that evening. So Eden motored to
London and saw Maisky at the Foreign Office that morning.
Maisky told Eden he felt sure that Hitler would accompany his
attack on Russia with peace overtures to the West and he
seemed anxious for an assurance that there would be no
slackening of the British war effort. Eden readily gave one.

Meanwhile, Churchill had been preparing his statement to
the nation. He started on it immediately after breakfast and he
remained in his bedroom, busily engaged on it, most of the
morning. After lunch he went out into the garden, taking his
papers with him. There was a seat set in the shelter of a semi-
circular yew hedge, and it was here that Churchill liked to sit
on fine afternoons and read or dictate. Ever and anon, however,
he would get up and walk across to the rose garden, declaiming
all the time. The result of all this preparation was one of the
most famous of all Churchill's wartime speeches. It was delivered
from the Hawtrey Room immediately after the nine o'clock
news. The Prime Minister said:

> I have taken occasion to speak to you tonight because we have
> reached one of the climacterics of the war. . . . At four o'clock this
> morning Hitler attacked and invaded Russia. . . .
> Hitler is a monster of wickedness, insatiable in his lust for blood
> and plunder. Not content with having all Europe under his heel,
> or else terrorized into various forms of abject submission, he must
> now carry his work of butchery and desolation among the vast
> multitudes of Russia and Asia. The terrible military machine,
> which we and the rest of the civilised world so foolishly, so
> supinely, so insensately allowed the Nazi gangsters to build up
> year by year from almost nothing, cannot stand idle lest it rust or
> fall to pieces. It must be in continual motion, grinding up human
> lives and trampling down the homes and the rights of hundreds of
> millions of men. Moreover it must be fed, not only with flesh but
> with oil.
> So now this bloodthirsty guttersnipe must launch his mechan-
> ized armies upon new fields of slaughter, pillage and devastation.

Poor as are the Russian peasants, workmen and soldiers, he must steal from them their daily bread; he must devour their harvests; he must rob them of the oil which drives their ploughs; and thus produce a famine without example in human history. And even the carnage and ruin which his victory, should he gain it – he has not gained it yet – will bring upon the Russian people, will itself be only a stepping-stone to the attempt to plunge the four or five hundred millions who live in China, and the three hundred and fifty millions who live in India, into that bottomless pit of human degradation over which the diabolic emblem of the Swastika flaunts itself. It is not too much to say, here this summer evening, that the lives and happiness of a thousand million additional people are now menaced with brutal Nazi violence. . . .

But now I have to declare the decision of His Majesty's Government – and I feel sure it is a decision in which the great Dominions will, in due course, concur – for we must speak out now at once, without a day's delay. I have to make the declaration, but can you doubt what our policy will be? We have but one aim and one single, irrevocable purpose. We are resolved to destroy Hitler and every vestige of the Nazi regime. From this nothing will turn us – nothing. We will never parley, we will never negotiate with Hitler or any of his gang. We shall fight him by land, we shall fight him by sea, we shall fight him in the air, until with God's help we have rid the earth of his shadow and liberated its people from his yoke. Any man or state who fights on against Nazidom will have our aid. Any man or state who marches with Hitler is our foe. . . .

It follows, therefore, that we shall give whatever help we can to Russia and the Russian people. We shall appeal to all our friends and allies in every part of the world to take the same course and pursue it, as we shall, faithfully and steadfastly to the end. . . .

We shall bomb Germany by day as well as by night in ever-increasing measure, casting upon them month by month a heavier discharge of bombs, and making the German people taste and gulp each month a sharper dose of the miseries they have showered upon mankind. . . .

This is no class war, but a war in which the whole British Empire and Commonwealth of Nations is engaged without distinction of race, creed or party. It is not for me to speak of the action of the United States, but this I will say: if Hitler imagines that his attack on Soviet Russia will cause the slightest division of aims or slackening of effort in the great Democracies who are resolved upon his doom, he is woefully mistaken. On the contrary, we shall be fortified and encouraged in our efforts to rescue mankind from his tyranny. . . . The Russian danger is therefore our danger, and the danger of the United States, just as the cause of any Russian fighting for his hearth and home is the cause of free men and free peoples in every quarter of the globe. Let us learn the lessons already taught by such cruel experience. Let us redouble our exertions, and strike with united strength while life and power remain.

That same evening, discussing the situation with Winant and Dill (Chief of the Imperial General Staff), Churchill expressed confidence in the Russians' will and power to resist.

Early in July 1941 the American Embassy in London received the following cable from the White House: "To Winant from Roosevelt: please tell former naval person to expect Hopkins very soon." The President had scribbled out this message on the back of a map of the Atlantic which he had torn from the *National Geographic Magazine*. Roosevelt was agreeably surprised by the strength and duration of the Russians' resistance, which had already gone on longer than many of his experts had thought likely, and he wanted to help them in any way that he could. But he wanted to make sure that such aid as he felt he could afford to give was of the right kind and as effective as possible. Churchill was delighted when he heard that Hopkins was coming.

Hopkins had left Washington a day or two before very early in the morning. He flew to Montreal and then to Gander and from there in a Lend Lease B24 Bomber to Prestwick in Scotland. He was very ill when he got there, but in spite of this he went straight on to London, going to Downing Street as soon as he arrived there. He was welcomed by Churchill, who invited him to attend a Cabinet meeting.

That weekend Hopkins went to Chequers. The weather was good, and on this occasion, he did not have to wear his overcoat at all. He had brought with him the page from the magazine containing the map of the Atlantic, across which Roosevelt had drawn a line indicating the route which convoys might be expected to take on their way to Russia and the respective sea lanes for which the British and U.S. navies might assume responsibility. All this he explained to Churchill, who was deeply interested.

On the Saturday (19th July) there was a large lunch party at

Chequers and Hopkins was one of the guests. When the meal was over they all moved into the White Parlour for coffee, where, in spite of the good weather, Mrs Churchill, out of consideration for Hopkins, had had a fire lit. In the course of the afternoon the Soviet Ambassador arrived at Chequers. Maisky had decided to deliver personally a message addressed by Stalin to Churchill which had recently reached the Russian embassy. On his arrival, Maisky was taken into the White Parlour, where the lunch guests were still assembled. Churchill immediately left the others and took the ambassador into his study. After reading carefully through Stalin's message, which called for the immediate inception of a second front in Northern France or the Arctic, Churchill said, "I quite understand Monsieur Stalin and sympathize with him deeply, but unfortunately what he asks is impracticable." He then explained the reasons for this at considerable length. Maisky argued with him but to no avail.

They then returned to the White Parlour, where for the first time Maisky met Hopkins, to whom he was introduced by Churchill. Hopkins was standing in front of the fire, and Churchill said to him, "Here is Stalin asking for the creation of a second front in France. We can't do it at present. We are not strong enough." The Prime Minister then moved away to talk to his other guests, while Maisky remained by the fire with Hopkins. They got on well together. The ambassador soon found, as others had, that behind Hopkins' emaciated appearance there was a keen intellect and a strong will. Soon, however, Mrs Churchill announced that tea was ready in the Great Hall, and Maisky did not feel that this was a suitable moment for further serious discussions with Hopkins. He left Chequers soon afterwards, but the two men met again the following week, and Maisky broached the idea of a visit by Hopkins to Moscow. It is probable that the same idea had already occurred to Hopkins himself. One of the objects of his journey to England had been to pave the way for a meeting between Roosevelt and Churchill. Hopkins knew that he would be present at this meeting and that Russia's needs would be among the most important matters to be discussed, and it was this which made him particularly keen to go there.

Hopkins was again at Chequers the following weekend (25th

to 27th July). He found Churchill also extremely keen on the idea of him going to Russia and a message was sent to the White House asking for the President's approval. It was at Chequers, late on the evening of Saturday 26th July, that Hopkins received Roosevelt's reply. "Welles and I highly approve Moscow trip and assume you would go in a few days," the President said.

Meanwhile Churchill had invited Hopkins to broadcast to the nation the following evening (Sunday) after the nine o'clock news. It so happened that that particular weekend all the guests (apart from Lindemann) were Americans. Among them was Quentin Reynolds, a journalist whose writings and broadcasts had greatly pleased Churchill. For lunch on the first day there was smoked salmon followed by meat. After taking a few mouthfuls of the latter, Churchill said, "This isn't lamb; it's mutton. Clemmie, can't you get us better meat than this?" She smiled and said, "Remember, Winston there is a war on." Later she made some remark about his consumption of alcohol, and he said, "Always remember, Clemmie, that I have taken more out of alcohol than alcohol has taken out of me."

Hopkins knew what a success Reynolds' broadcasts had been, and he invited him to help him with his own. Reynolds promised to do so. During lunch, Mrs Churchill made several references to Hopkins' health, and he, according to Reynolds, "gave me a despairing look which suggested that he had been receiving some excessive mothering since his arrival in England". Hopkins had been working very long hours and was undoubtedly showing signs of strain. He was tired out and told Mrs Churchill that he thought he "had a touch of grippe". She and Mrs Roosevelt were both solicitous of him, especially Mrs Churchill, who by then knew him so well that she could tell when he was in pain. Churchill always wanted to keep him up late, but around eleven o'clock in the evening, Mrs Churchill would start trying to get him off to bed, saying, "You have a long day tomorrow and you can have a nice talk with Winston in the morning. I'll fix your bed and put a hot water bottle in it."

This was the first time that Reynolds had been to Chequers, and he found, as others did, that Churchill grew in stature in these more intimate surroundings and that it was impossible not to be impressed by his aura of strength even when chatting about trivialities. The whole burden of preserving the world seemed to rest on his shoulders, but he gave no sign of strain. His private conversation was at times oddly suggestive of his public speeches – the same beautifully turned phrases and the same use of alliteration and repetition. "Now we are getting stronger," he would say, "and that evil man Hitler knows it. He knows his days are numbered, even at this moment when his submarines are sinking our vessels in the North Atlantic, even now when his planes are bombing this island. . . ." Reynolds asked him what sort of a world it would be after the war and he replied, "The same old world with a bit of the gingerbread knocked off."

When lunch was over, Hopkins and Reynolds went up into the former's bedroom to prepare the broadcast. Hopkins threw himself down on the bed and then told Reynolds in broad outline what he wanted to say. He explained that "Anything I say will be construed as a direct message from F.D.R. People know I'm only the President's messenger boy." He added that, though he wanted to give the British people as much hope as possible, he "couldn't be too specific". After Hopkins had said all he had to say, Reynolds sat down at a typewriter which had been provided for Hopkins' use and started to type, while Hopkins remained on the bed, playing with Nelson, the Prime Minister's cat. When he had finished typing, Reynolds read over his draft to Hopkins, who, however, exclaimed, "Hell, Quent you've got me declaring war on Germany." To this Reynolds replied: "We should have done that long ago." They then had to start all over again. The finished product was delivered from the Hawtrey Room by Hopkins over Churchill's own microphone at about 9.15 on Sunday evening 27th July. Here, with the portraits of the Hawtreys in their Elizabethan attire and of Sir Francis Bacon looking down on him, Harry Hopkins (as reported in *The Times*) said:

> I have been with the President when messages came to him telling him of the bombing of workers' flats in the East End of London. I was with him when the news came of the tragic bombing of Coventry and later of Plymouth. I heard the words which came not from his lips only but from his heart as well. I watched the stern development of his determination to beat Hitler. The President is at one with your Prime Minister in his determination

to break the ruthless power of that sinful psychopathic in Berlin.

The President asked me to come over here. My instructions were: "Find out if the material we are sending to Britain is arriving. Find out if it is what Britain wants. Let me know if there is anything more Britain needs." This is my mission. I have found out the things he asked me to find out. . . . I have learnt from your Cabinet Ministers what England needs now and I am returning to America to report this to the President. . . . No enemy action can stop the ceaseless tide of ships coming here daily, this time laden with something more substantial than hopes and sympathy. During the past several months aeroplanes now numbering in the thousands made in American factories have been flown or shipped across the Atlantic. . . . America has already sent several hundred tanks throughout the Empire; many more are on the way. . . . And yet we realize that our part to date has not been great. Our contribution has been but a modest part in your great war effort. . . . It took some time to realize that the war might well be decided in the factories of Detroit, of Los Angeles, in the steel mills of Pittsburgh and in the mines of Pennsylvania. . . . That is now being realized. . . . Today American industry joins hands with the men who work for Beaverbrook and Bevin in forgetting factional trade union disputes, in limiting holidays, in sacrificing for the common victory.

We have not neglected the question of food. America will never allow the people of Britain to go hungry. America has decided to decrease consumption of food and to increase production. During the next twelve months huge quantities [of food] will arrive here. A thousand miscellaneous articles, all important to the war effort, are being produced and are on their way. . . . Your Prime Minister asked us for the tools. I promise you that they are coming; that an endless assembly belt stretches from our western coast to this island and to the middle east; that nothing will be allowed to interfere with the full efficiency of this supply line. . . . President Roosevelt promised that he will take steps to ensure the delivery of goods consigned to Britain. . . . Our President does not give his word lightly. . . . Tonight British and American warships are patrolling on parallel lanes with only one object – to guard the world's lifeline. Even now, as I speak, sleek grey destroyers flying the American flag are plunging their way through the waters of the North Atlantic.

People of England, people of Britain, people of the British Commonwealth of nations – you are not fighting alone.

It had taken Hopkins longer than he had anticipated to deliver this address, and he knew that he would have to leave immediately if he was to catch his train. But Churchill insisted on taking him out into the garden for a stroll and a final talk. It was a fine evening and not yet completely dark. The Prime Minister talked in considerable detail about his plans for bringing aid to Russia and of the importance which he attached to that country in the struggle to overthrow Hitler. Hopkins asked if he could repeat some of this to Stalin. "Tell him," said Churchill, "tell him that Britain has but one ambition today – to crush Hitler. Tell him that he can depend on us. . . . Goodbye – God bless you Harry."

A few minutes later, Hopkins was speeding through the Buckinghamshire lanes with Averell Harriman in whose car he was being driven to Euston station, where he would board a train for Invergordon in Scotland. Thence he was to be flown by a R.A.F. Catalina to Archangel. The colloquy with Churchill had made them late, and they had to drive very fast to catch the train. They only just managed it. Hopkins had no time to go back to Claridges, where he had been staying, to pay the bill; he did not do so until six weeks later. A member of the embassy staff had been sent there to collect his scanty belongings, and these were delivered to him at the station. Just as the train was pulling out, the American Ambassador came running down the platform with Hopkins' passport, containing a visa which Maisky had written out in his own handwriting. Winant managed to hand it to Hopkins through the carriage window while the train was actually moving. He need not have taken the trouble. The Russians never asked to see Hopkins' passport. He had recently been favoured with some attention from Dr Goebbels, whose propaganda had resulted in greatly increasing Hopkins' prestige with the Russians.

Rather over a fortnight later, on a fine Sunday morning in August, Churchill was out and about at Chequers unusually early. He had got up soon after breakfast. The staff knew he was going away – leaving shortly before lunch – but they did not know his destination. He was in excellent humour and evidently very excited. He seemed unwilling to sit down but kept walking up and down the Great Hall and from room to room and then out into the garden. Finally he could restrain his impatience no longer, and shortly before one o'clock he ordered the car to take him to Princes Risborough Station, though it was still too early for the train. This involved a long wait which he spent pacing up and down the platform. Ultimately the long special train, with restaurant and sleeping cars, which had left Addison Road that morning, drew in to the Buckinghamshire station. The rest of the party were on board. The passengers, some of whom had accompanied the Prime Minister from Chequers, included Sir Alexander Cadogan of the Foreign Office, Lord Cherwell, the First Sea Lord (Admiral Pound), the C.I.G.S. (Field Marshal Dill), the Vice-Chief of Air Staff (Sir W. Freeman), Colonels Hollis and Jacobs of the Defence Office, Commander Thompson and other members of Churchill's personal staff, as well as a retinue of officers of the technical and administrative branches of the Plans Division and a considerable number of cyphering experts.

As soon as the train left an excellent lunch was served, accompanied by champagne. They travelled all through the night and the next morning reached the Orkneys, where they boarded a destroyer which took them to Scapa Flow, where the battleship *Prince of Wales* was awaiting them. Here, too, they found Harry Hopkins, who had arrived two days before on his return from Moscow, tired and ill. In the hurry of his departure from England he had forgotten to take with him the medicines and injections which his doctor considered essential. As soon as he got on board the *Prince of Wales* he was put straight to bed, on the admiral's instructions. Winant had flown specially to Scotland to bid the party farewell and he talked to the admiral and the ship's doctor, who both promised to look after Hopkins.

Just before they left Scapa Flow, Churchill sent a message to Roosevelt to say: "Harry returned from Russia dead beat but is lively again now. We shall get him in fine trim on the voyage. We are just off. . . . Look forward so much to our meeting. Kindest regards." Then the battleship put to sea and bore them to a quiet bay off Newfoundland, where President and Prime Minister met and, in due course, signed the Atlantic Charter.

In October 1941 there arrived at Chequers a young naval officer who was to be a frequent visitor there during the next two years. This was Captain Lord Louis Mountbatten, later to become Admiral of the Fleet the Earl Mountbatten of Burma.

A few weeks previously he had been commanding the aircraft carrier *Illustrious* in the Pacific, and he had not been best pleased at receiving Churchill's summons to return to England immediately, particularly as this had involved refusing an invitation from Roosevelt to visit him at the White House.

When Mountbatten arrived at Chequers Churchill took him into his study and then told him why he had been sent for. "You will take over command of Combined Operations from Admiral Keyes," the Prime Minister said to him. "You will continue commando raids as they are so important for the morale of this country and of our allies. But your primary object will be to prepare for the great invasion, for unless we return to the continent and beat the Germans on land we shall never win the war. All the other headquarters in this country are thinking *defensively*. Your job will be to think *offensively* – to restore the offensive spirit and devise the technique and find the appliances and landing craft which will be needed."

Mountbatten was not at all pleased when he heard this. He would much rather have remained where he was, fighting with his friends at sea; a shore job was the last thing he wanted at that particular moment. He was unable to conceal his feelings from Churchill, who turned to him angrily and said, "Have you no sense of history? Don't you want the job?" "No, Prime Minister, I don't," replied Mountbatten. "I've just taken on a new command – the *Illustrious*, and I don't want an office job. I'd rather go back to sea." Churchill's retort was: "Have you no sense of glory? I offer you participation in the highest leadership in the war and all you want to do is to go back to sea. What could you hope to achieve except to be sunk in a bigger and more expensive battleship?"

Mountbatten saw that it was no use arguing with Churchill once his mind was made up, so he threw himself into his new job. He went frequently to Chequers, where he and Churchill would spend many hours after dinner smoking cigars and drinking brandy and discussing some favourite new project. Churchill undoubtedly liked Mountbatten. They had much in common. Both were men of great courage and personality, both were dynamic, both were intensely receptive to new ideas, and both had scant respect for officialdom. It was fatally easy for a serving officer to be lured down to Chequers and then, over the champagne or brandy, to be persuaded to agree or seem to agree with one of Churchill's favourite projects, only to be confronted with his agreement or apparent agreement before the chiefs of staff a day or two later. Mountbatten was well aware of this danger, and he guarded against it. He showed great prescience and tact in preparing for the chiefs of staff a full report of all his conversations at Chequers.

There was an idea which was given the code name 'Habbakuk' on which Churchill and Mountbatten were both keen, though there was a certain scepticism about it at the Admiralty. It took the form of a million-ton aircraft carrier consisting of a mobile, artificially constructed iceberg, on which aircraft could land and take off in mid-ocean. The difficulty was to prevent the ice from melting, but Geoffrey Pyke, one of Mountbatten's staff, believed that a solution had been found in the form of a substance which was called 'Pykrete' after its inventor. It consisted of 5 per cent waste paper or pulp and 95 per cent sea water. So excited was Mountbatten about this that he rushed straight off to Chequers, taking a small sample of 'Pykrete' with him. When he got there and demanded to see the Prime Minister immediately, he was told by Sawyers, the butler, that Churchill was having a bath. "Excellent," said Mountbatten, "he couldn't be in a better place," and, hastily mounting the stairs, he burst into the bathroom and, after one or two brief words of introduction, flung the 'Pykrete' into the bath. The result was to turn the water slightly cold and this, in the first instance, did not please the Prime Minister at all. But when Mountbatten turned on the hot tap and showed that the 'Pykrete' hardly melted, Churchill became deeply interested and thereafter he was a keen advocate of both 'Habbakuk' and 'Pykrete'. The idea was only abandoned when Portugal allowed the allies to use the Azores as a mid-Atlantic air base for anti-U-boat warfare.

Mountbatten believed whenever possible in personally testing new weapons or devices which were under consideration by his staff. One of these was the Wellman one-man submarine for use in small scale raids on enemy shipping, which the Admiralty had turned down. One of these had been sent for trial to Staines reservoir. While staying for the weekend at Chequers, Mount-

The Long Gallery

Lord and Lady Lee of Fareham

batten decided to go over to Staines on the Sunday morning to attend the trials, and when he got there he insisted on trying it out himself. At a depth of about twenty feet the glass scuttle in front of him started to leak and water squirted out on to his face and clothes. However he managed to surface and when he was safely ashore expressed himself in forceful language about this defect. When he got back to Chequers he had to change his clothes and in making his excuses to the Prime Minister gave him a description of the incident which he seemed to think was rather funny. But Churchill was not at all amused. On the contrary, he administered a severe rebuke, telling Mountbatten that now that he was a member of the Chiefs of Staffs Committee he had "no business to be fooling about with one-man submarines in person". In October 1943 Mountbatten became Supreme Allied Commander South-east Asia and ceased therefore to be a regular visitor to Chequers.

Meanwhile, whether they realized it or not, Roosevelt's and Hopkins' days as unofficial allies of Britain and Russia were numbered. So far as American neutrality was concerned, the sands of time were fast running out. In the summer of 1940 Japan had signed the tripartite pact with Germany and Italy, but so far she had not followed this up by any overt act. In October 1941 the moderate Prince Konoye was succeeded as Prime Minister by the militant and aggressive General Tojo. As usual, Churchill saw what this meant sooner than almost anyone else. In a speech at the Mansion House on 10th November he said, "Should the United States become involved in war with Japan the British declaration will follow within the hour." He could not, however, be sure that the converse would apply and this was one of his many anxieties. At the end of November the American intelligence intercepted a message sent by the Japanese government to Berlin that war in the Far East might break out quicker than anyone supposed. But this was quite consistent with the initial attack being made on British possessions only. The Japanese behaved with great treachery and deceit and continued their negotiations with the Americans while their fleet was on the way to Pearl Harbour.

It was quite a small party which assembled at Chequers on the evening of the first Friday in December 1941, and the

I

atmosphere was distinctly gloomy. Mrs Churchill was not feeling at all well, and this was an added source of anxiety for the Prime Minister. Averell Harriman came on the Saturday and Winant on the Sunday. Both were to stay to dinner on the Sunday night. But the presence of these two distinguished Americans, both of whom he liked, failed to cheer up the Prime Minister.

Winant had spent the night before as the guest of Anthony Eden at the latter's home in Sussex. He had been very tired when he got there, and he and Eden had stayed up till very late. They had had much to talk about. The next morning (Sunday) Eden had had to leave early as he was going to Moscow, but he suggested that Winant should stay on and rest; Mrs Eden and his (Eden's) brother would be there, he explained. But Winant was worried about reports he had received concerning Japanese activities and he said he wanted to see the Prime Minister at once. So they telephoned to Chequers.

When Winant arrived there, after a long drive, he found Churchill pacing up and down outside the front door. The Prime Minister immediately asked the ambassador whether he thought there was going to be war with Japan, and, on receiving an affirmative answer, declared vehemently, "If they declare war on you we shall declare war on them within the hour." "I understand that, Prime Minister," came the reply, "you have said so publicly." Then Churchill gave expression to the doubt which was worrying him most of all. "If they declare war on us," he asked, "will you declare war on them?" "I can't answer that, Prime Minister," said Winant, "only the Congress has the right to declare war under the Constitution of the United States." Churchill was silent for a minute or two. Then he turned to his guest and said, "We're late you know. You get washed and then we'll go in to lunch together."

When the meal was over, Churchill did a little work in his study and then, as was his wont, went up to his bedroom to rest. Harriman, Winant and Harriman's daughter Kathie decided to go out for a walk. To all outward semblance these two American statesmen were strongly contrasted. Winant was tall and imposing looking; Harriman was neither. It has been said that he "had the curious contempt for elegance that only the wealthy can afford". He was a multi-millionaire, the son of a thrusting ruthless American businessman who had made an enormous fortune out of railroads. Harriman was a Democrat; Winant was or until recently had been a Republican. Both had come to England earlier that year – Harriman as Roosevelt's specially appointed envoy, Winant as ambassador. Of Harriman it has been written that "the United States never had a more devoted servant". Much the same could have been said with equal truth of the other forthright American who strode by his side across the Buckinghamshire fields and through the beech woods that winter afternoon. But each had made it his business also to study closely the needs of England.

Dinner, as usual, was late that evening, and it was nearly nine o'clock before the party entered the dining room. It was noticed that the Prime Minister was unusually taciturn. Just before nine o'clock Sawyers came into the room and put Churchill's portable wireless set on a small table by his elbow. This set had been given to the Prime Minister by Harry Hopkins. It was several minutes before Churchill noticed that it was there, and when he did so the nine o'clock news had already started. Alvar Liddell was reading it, and just after Churchill turned on the set the announcer was heard to say something about air attacks on the Hawaiian Islands. Then he went on to talk about a tank battle south of Tobruk, but Churchill suddenly sat up and said, "Didn't he say something about an attack on an American base?" Sawyers said that he had heard it too. Meanwhile the narrator had started to deal with the Russian front and with R.A.F. activities. But then suddenly there was a change in his voice. "I have just heard," he said, "that Japanese aircraft have raided Pearl Harbour, the American naval base in Hawaii. The announcement of the attack was made in a brief statement by President Roosevelt. Naval and military targets on the principal Hawaiian Island of Oahu have also been attacked. No further details are yet available." Immediately Churchill got up and said, "We will declare war on Japan," at the same time starting for the door. Winant immediately followed him. "Good God," he said, "you can't declare war on a radio announcement." The ambassador then suggested that they should get through to the President, and within a few minutes the White House was on the line. Winant spoke to Roosevelt first and then said there was someone else who wanted to speak to him, adding "you will know who it is as soon as you hear his voice". A second or two later Roosevelt and Churchill were talking to one another. "It's quite true," said the President, "they have attacked us at Pearl Harbour. We're all in the same boat now." The next day he spoke to a joint session of Congress of "a day which will live in infamy" and said, "No matter how long it may take us to overcome this premeditated invasion the American people in their righteous might will win through to ultimate victory. . . . With confidence in our armed forces, with the unbounded determination of our people we will gain the inevitable triumph, so help us God."

Meanwhile, that Sunday evening at Chequers, shortly after finishing his conversation with Roosevelt, Churchill was again called to the telephone. This time it was to talk to Eden, who was at Invergordon and about to board a destroyer for Murmansk. He had just heard the news. Churchill told him he had decided to go to Washington. Eden asked whether he should put off his Russian visit and come too, but Churchill told him to adhere to his arrangements and to go to Russia. Winant also spoke to Eden. And the following telegram was sent to Harry Hopkins: "Thinking of you much at this historic moment – Winston Averell."

Far into the night and into the small hours of the following morning, Churchill sat up at Chequers drafting messages and reading telegrams as they were decoded. Winant and Harriman helped him. There was a great deal to do. Telephone calls were put through to the Foreign Office regarding the forthcoming declaration of war on Japan. Parliament was not due to meet until the following Tuesday, and telephone calls had therefore also to be put through to the Speaker and the Whips. Directions were given for M.P.s to be recalled the following day (Monday), and the unprecedented step was taken of doing this by wireless. It was even later than usual when Churchill got to bed. There is no doubt that the news had brought him feelings of relief, joy and thankfulness. So great was his knowledge of and confidence in the power and might of the United States that he was now quite certain that Britain and America would win the war and

this conviction stirred up in him a strong emotion. When at last
the time came to go to bed, he "slept the sleep of the saved and
the thankful".

It was a very quiet Christmas at Chequers that year – the
first for four years when there was no Prime Minister there, for
Churchill was spending it at the White House. As he accompanied the President at the lighting of the Christmas tree on the
White House lawn, Churchill told the world that "I spend this
anniversary and festival far from my country, far from my
family yet I cannot say that I feel really far from home . . . here
in the centre and at the summit of the United States."

About the middle of April 1942, Harry Hopkins once more
arrived at Chequers. He was feeling much better this time. He
had had a comparatively comfortable journey over by Pan
American clipper, and they had broken the journey in Bermuda,
where Harry and his party had spent two days of very pleasant
rest. In England the weather was good, and during the last part
of the drive from London to Chequers, on a fine Saturday afternoon in early spring, Hopkins was struck by the intense beauty
of the surrounding countryside. He said later that "It's only
when you see that country in spring that you understand why
the English have written the best goddam poetry in the world."

Churchill and Hopkins spent most of that evening talking
about India. A difference of opinion had arisen between
Churchill and Roosevelt on this matter. The President thought
that, with a Japanese invasion highly likely, every effort should
be made to gain Indian sympathy and stiffen their resistance to
the Japanese by giving them an immediate promise of early
home rule. The Prime Minister (and the British Cabinet), on
the other hand, felt that this was not the moment at which to
throw the whole sub-continent into the confusion which they
believed would result from such a step. In threshing out this
complex problem that evening at Chequers, Churchill kept
Hopkins up into the small hours of the following morning,
Sunday. At 3 a.m. a long cable came through to Chequers from
the White House. It was addressed to Hopkins and contained a
message from Roosevelt to Churchill, chiefly about Indian
affairs. Sir Stafford Cripps had recently been sent out to India
to try to achieve some kind of agreement with the Congress

Party but he had not found this possible. In his cable, Roosevelt asked that Cripps' return to England should be deferred and that still further efforts to reach agreement with the Congress Party should be made. In fact, Cripps was already on his way back to England.

Hopkins and Churchill stayed up for quite a long time after Roosevelt's message had been received. Then Hopkins managed to snatch a few hours' sleep. Immediately after breakfast on that Sunday he went down to the Secretary's room and tried to telephone the White House. But the atmospheric conditions were so bad that he was unable to get through. Several hours later he did manage to get on to the President and explained that Cripps had already left India. He also evidently managed to convey to the President an idea of the hour and the conditions in which his (Roosevelt's) cable had arrived at Chequers and of the length of the nocturnal discussion. The following morning, there arrived in London the following cable from the President addressed this time to General Marshall: "Please put Hopkins to bed and keep him there under twenty-four hour guard by army or Marine corps. Ask the King for additional assistance if required on this job."

In May 1942 Chequers received its first important Russian visitors, the delegation being led by Molotov, Soviet Foreign Secretary. They had asked to be provided with accommodation in the country; Churchill had immediately decided to put Chequers at their disposal, and they were there for about a week. The Prime Minister himself remained in London, but came down twice to Chequers during their visit and had important talks with Molotov.

The Russians had flown to Scotland, where a reception committee led by Sir Alexander Cadogan had met them. One of their planes (a Russian Flamingo) had crashed, the Russian air attaché and three others being killed. The remainder of the party were all late, and Molotov's aircraft landed at an airfield several miles away from its intended destination. A special train conveyed the visitors from Scotland to Wendover station, where Commander Thompson, a member of Churchill's personal staff was waiting for them. The staff at Chequers had been told that there would be six visitors, but in fact about twenty (including

Maisky) disembarked at Wendover and insisted on being driven
to Chequers, where they all evidently had every intention of
stopping for that and the ensuing nights. A Guard of Honour
was drawn up outside the house and Molotov was invited to
inspect it. Maisky appears to have suggested to Molotov that he
should give the 'V sign' and Molotov attempted to do so but
pointed his fingers in the wrong direction greatly to the amusement of the Guard, who had difficulty in keeping straight faces.

The visit looked like being a nightmare for the staff. Dinner
had been prepared for twelve but it now looked as though the
Russians alone would be more than twenty, and it was doubtful
whether there would be enough food. To add to the confusion,
the guests, when shown to their rooms, refused to enter them
until they had received permission to do so from Molotov. There
was a heated argument resolved ultimately by Maisky, who
arranged for fourteen of his fellow countrymen to return to
London after dinner. Those who remained demanded keys for
their rooms, which they invariably locked on leaving so that the
regular staff were confronted with great difficulty in getting
access to them for the purpose of making the beds and doing the
cleaning. When at last they did so, they were surprised and
alarmed to find pistols under the pillows. The three chief
members of the mission were attended not only by police officers
but by two women servants each. These latter not only looked
after their clothes and tidied up the rooms, but also, when the
delegates were away from them, maintained a constant watch
over the rooms, only going down to meals one at a time. In the
case of Molotov himself, the precautions were carried still
further. Every nook and cranny of the room was made the
subject of an intensive search by the Russian police. The bed-
clothes were thoroughly prodded and the sheets rearranged so
as to make it easier for the occupant to leap out of bed in the
event of a nocturnal attack. Molotov's own behaviour was
entirely in keeping with all this. On one occasion, the curator,
Miss Lamont, observing a light on in the middle of the night in
spite of the 'black out', went to the door of the room from which
it appeared to be coming and, on endeavouring to gain access,
was confronted by Molotov with a loaded revolver.

During his visit, which lasted for more than a week, Molotov drove every morning to London. No one knew what time he would be back and this made the catering arrangements extremely difficult as different times for his return were given by the Russian embassy throughout the day. Sometimes he did not get back until around midnight, by which time the dinner prepared for him was completely ruined. At breakfast the secretaries generally came down first, but as soon as Molotov appeared they dashed from the room, whether they had had anything to eat or not. Now and again, in the afternoon, to help to pass the time, Thompson and Geoffrey Wilson, the interpreter sent to Chequers for the visit, would try to teach some of the Russians how to play croquet. It was noticed that one of the secretaries always brought his brief case with him and would never let it out of his possession for more than a minute or two. It became clear, in due course, that a number of the Russians were not what they appeared to be. One of the 'typists' hardly ever left her room and, though if anyone was within eye or ear-shot she would pretend to be manipulating her machine, it soon became clear that she was unable to type. Molotov's personal 'servant' turned out later to be an important Russian general. No one was able to discover the reason for these strange proceedings.

In the course of his talks with Molotov at Chequers, Churchill did his best to explain his ideas on strategy and to emphasize the difficulties inherent in amphibious warfare. He gave a farewell dinner party for them the night before their departure, when the menu included quail specially produced for the occasion. They had, however, been in cold storage for an unduly long time, and the Prime Minister's comment was that, "These miserable mice should never have been removed from Tutankhamen's tomb."

In February 1943, after returning from the Casablanca conference, Churchill became extremely ill. He had contracted a feverish cold and inflammation of the lung set in, and this was later followed by pneumonia. He made a good recovery, however, and went to Chequers for ten days to convalesce. During this time, he was twice visited there by the King. It was while he was at Chequers that he prepared the broadcast on post-war policy which he made in March 1943, and he invited R. A. Butler down there to go through it with him.

The names of British admirals, generals and air marshals are of course, very much to the fore in that part of the visitors' book which relates to the war period – Dowding, Portal, Brooke, Pound, Cunningham, Slesson, Daniel, Harris, Wavell, Dill, Pile, Sholto Douglas, Auchinleck, Mountbatten, Portal, Joubert, Peck, Ismay, Montgomery, to mention only a few. The names of the Commanders-in-Chief of Bomber and Fighter Command are particularly noticeable during the early days; they were often invited to dine and sometimes to stay at Chequers, the first to do so being Sir Hugh Dowding, Commander-in-Chief Fighter Command at the outbreak of war. He it was who had persuaded Churchill not to accede to the French request that the whole Metropolitan Air Force should be thrown into the Battle of France. By this advice, Dowding had contributed in no small measure to the winning of the Battle of Britain, and Churchill, no doubt recognizing this, gave him a particularly warm welcome on the occasion of his early visits to Chequers. His last visit there in November 1941 was less happy, however. He had been retired from his Command but had written a book about the future conduct of the war and the peace which was to follow it which Churchill had promised to read. After dinner when Dowding started to talk about his book, however, Churchill kept getting up and walking about the room, playing songs on the gramophone and joining in the chorus.

Dowding's successor, Sholto Douglas, was also invited to Chequers more than once and was fascinated by the "unaffected and warm-hearted delight" which Churchill displayed in the presents showered on him from all over the world, including cigars and magnums of champagne, many of which found their way to Chequers. Hard by, at High Wycombe, was the headquarters of Bomber Command, and its chief would often motor over for dinner with the Prime Minister to get further backing for the bomber offensive in which Churchill and Lindemann were both great believers.

Air Marshal Harris would sometimes arrive wearing a plum-coloured velveteen dinner jacket. Harris was one of the few service chiefs in whose company Churchill occasionally allowed himself to relax and talk about subjects other than the war. One

evening in February 1944, for instance, when the party at
Chequers included Harris, they went up into the Long Gallery
after dinner and listened to the music of *The Mikado* and
Churchill said that it brought back his youth and the Victorian
era – "eighty years which will rank in our island history with the
Antonines". Harris always received a particularly warm welcome when he went to Chequers. His enthusiasm for and
successes in the bombing of Germany had greatly pleased
Churchill. Driving back through the Buckinghamshire countryside after these encounters, Harris would hum to himself
"Malbrouk s'en va en guerre".

But the visitors to Chequers during the war years were by no
means exclusively serving officers. There were, of course, the
members of the Government, notably Lindemann, Cripps,
Bevin, Beaverbrook and Bracken; and, turning over the pages
of the visitors' book for this period, we find also the names of
people as widely different in personality avocation and back-,
ground as Robin Maugham, Alexander Korda, J. L. Garvin
and the Duke of Marlborough. Eleanor Roosevelt went to
Chequers in 1942 and liked it. She was particularly interested
in the many traces which the place revealed of her Uncle,
Theodore Roosevelt, of whom she had been very fond and a
great admirer and who, being then the President, had given her
away on the occasion of her marriage in March 1905 to his fifth
cousin, Franklin D. Roosevelt. Watching the Prime Minister
playing on the floor with his grandson at Chequers, Mrs
Roosevelt was struck by the "extraordinary resemblance"
between the two. But Churchill told her he did not think his
grandson looked in the least like him but "just like other babies".

Of the distinguished military men who came to Chequers
from other lands during the war, two were destined later to go
into politics and rise to the supreme position in their own
countries. They were Charles de Gaulle and Dwight D.
Eisenhower.

De Gaulle went to Chequers quite a lot in the early days of
the war but he did not always sign the visitors' book. He went
there for lunch on 12th December 1940, when he disagreed
completely with Churchill that we were fighting the Nazis
rather than the Germans. *"Il y a toujours le militarisme allemand,"*

THE GREATEST OF THEM ALL

De Gaulle said. He went again for the weekend in February 1941. On this occasion he was accompanied by Madame de Gaulle. During this visit, de Gaulle and Churchill had an argument about Dakar. The conversations between them took place in French, Churchill's use of which language caused some amusement to his guests.

The American general presented a striking contrast to the Frenchman.

Churchill had first met Eisenhower in the United States in June 1942, and the following month Eisenhower arrived in England having been appointed by Roosevelt Commander-in-Chief of the U.S. forces in Europe. He paid his first visit to Chequers on 19th July 1942, he and his Deputy, General Mark Clark, having been invited for the weekend. Clark later gave an interesting and amusing account of what took place.

"Churchill bounced out to meet us wearing a siren suit and carpet slippers and beaming happily," Clark wrote. "He led us down a winding path through the woods until we came to a secluded seat, when we sat down and talked about coming events." Churchill said that he was in favour of postponing cross-Channel operations and opening up in North Africa.

The American generals when invited to Chequers seem to have behaved to Churchill in a manner in which no British general would have dreamt of behaving. In the course of dinner Clark suddenly said to Churchill, "Where is your short snorter?" This apparently was a certificate of having flown the Atlantic, and the holder was supposed always to have it on him, failure to produce it on demand by a fellow holder involving a fine of one dollar or drinks all round. The Prime Minister being unable to do so, Clark immediately said, "All right, pay up."

"No," replied Churchill, "I have it somewhere, so I won't pay up." When the general pointed out, that, according to the rules, this was no excuse Churchill said, "I make my own rules in my own house. Here everyone has an hour to produce his bill." He then "went shuffling into another part of the house", muttering to himself, and shortly after returned triumphantly with the document in question.

That evening there was the usual film show after dinner. Several of the guards officers came in to watch the show, as was their wont, and they were introduced to the two American generals. When the film was over Churchill disappeared and returned shortly afterwards with an old rifle which dated apparently from the Boer War. "Gentlemen," said the Prime Minister, "I'll show you how we used to do things." And he proceeded to do some arms drill for their benefit.

The next day Eisenhower and Clark inspected the guard, and just as they were finishing doing so Churchill poked his head through his bedroom window and said, "Aren't they a fine body of men?"

Eisenhower went to Chequers again on 29th August, when he was once more accompanied by Clark. On this occasion plans for the campaign in North Africa were discussed in more detail. Eisenhower paid one or two more visits to Chequers after this before leaving England in November 1942 for Gibraltar to organize the Allied landings in North Africa. He did not return to England until January 1944, following his appointment as Supreme Commander Allied Expeditionary Force charged with carrying out the invasion of France and Germany. On his return to England his weekly lunches with the Prime Minister at Downing Street and occasional weekends at Chequers were resumed.

Eisenhower noticed, as others had, how Churchill, even in private conversation at Chequers, would employ the rhetorical phrases which he used in his speeches, while, even at meal times, if Eisenhower or any other important general were present, he would ignore the rest of the company and talk to him entirely about the war. Now (1944) it was the projected invasion of France that was uppermost in his thoughts. At first he was apprehensive. "When I think of the beaches of Normandy choked with the flower of British and American youth," he said on one occasion, "and when in my mind's eye I see the tides running with their blood, I have my doubts ... I have my doubts." But then he would add, "We are committed to this operation of war and we must all do our best to make it a success." Eisenhower reassured him, and, in the course of another of their talks, the Prime Minister said, "General, it is good for commanders to be optimistic, or else they would never win a battle. I must say to you, if by the time the snow flies you have established your thirty odd divisions, now in Britain, safely on the Normandy coast, and have the port of Cherbourg firmly in your grasp I will be the first to proclaim that this was a gigantic and wonderfully conducted military campaign." Then he went on, "If, in addition, you should have seized the port of Havre and have extended your holdings to the Cotentin peninsula and the mouth of the Seine I will proclaim that this is one of the finest operations in modern war." And he added, "If by Christmas you have succeeded in liberating our beloved Paris, if she can by that time regain her life of freedom and take her accustomed place as a centre of European culture and beauty, then I will proclaim that this operation is the most grandly conceived and best conducted known to the history of warfare." To this Eisenhower replied, "Mr Prime Minister, we expect to be on the borders of Germany by Christmas, pounding away at her defences. When that occurs, if Hitler has the slightest judgement or wisdom left, he will surrender unconditionally to avoid the complete destruction of Germany."

Eisenhower himself wrote appreciatively of Chequers in his memoirs. Some of his staff were not so complimentary. His secretary undoubtedly shared the general American aversion to the place and described it in her book as "the freezing cold house in the Chilterns".

Besides his formal visits, when he generally stayed over the weekend, Eisenhower, if he found himself in the district, would sometimes drop in uninvited for a brief talk with the Prime Minister. On one such occasion, after spending about ten minutes with Churchill, he was about to drive away when he was called back by the butler to sign the visitors' book.

There was another soldier statesman who came from overseas during those years. This was Field Marshal Smuts; but his greatest triumphs in both these fields belonged to the past rather than the future. Churchill was a great admirer of him (as Lloyd George had been) and got him down to Chequers whenever he could, and they had many long talks about the conduct of the war and the future of the world after it. Smuts liked to stride across the hilly country round Chequers and in the course of his walks would pass the memorial erected on the top of Coombe Hill to commemorate the British victory in the

South African War. From time to time, too, he would encounter Randag, and they would talk to one another in their native tongue; but, though they understood one another perfectly, Randag's Dutch was quite different from Smuts' Afrikaans. Noticing this Churchill told them one day that they were "talking double Dutch".

It was at Chequers that Smuts prepared the speech which, at Churchill's invitation, he made to both houses of Parliament in 1942. Mackenzie King, Prime Minister of Canada, also stayed at Chequers during the war, and he too prepared while staying there the speech which he also made to the same audience. Both speeches are still preserved among the Chequers archives.

By this time, only two of the Prime Ministers who had preceded Churchill at Chequers were still living. They were Lloyd George and Baldwin. Lloyd George had been to stay there with Churchill in June 1942. Earlier on Churchill had invited him to join the Government, but his general attitude had not been very co-operative. In the summer of 1941 he had written to Lee telling him that:

> I should have liked . . . to arrange a personal interchange of views as to the progress of this extraordinary – and still more extraordinarily conducted – war. . . . I have been specially anxious to have your views as to the steps taken by the government for increasing the production of food. Personally I think results up to the present have been very disappointing, and I find the agricultural community disgruntled. There is certainly none of the enthusiasm and efficiency which characterised your notable achievement in the last war.

Baldwin was never Churchill's guest at Chequers, but in July 1943 he was invited to lunch at 10 Downing Street, and he and Churchill talked together for nearly three hours, mainly about the war. During the last four years Baldwin had been subjected to a constant stream of vilification and abuse, which he had endured with quiet dignity. He was, however, a sad and rather lonely man. His talk with Churchill cheered him up a great deal. He said to Harold Nicolson afterwards, "I went out into Downing Street a happy man. Of course, it was partly because an old buffer like me enjoys feeling that he is still not entirely out of things. But it was also pure patriotic joy that my country at such a time should have found such a leader. The furnace of war has smelted all the base metal out of him."

There is no doubt that the result of the 1945 General Election came as a shock and a bitter blow to Churchill. Until the last day or two he had been optimistic. Smuts had spent the weekend at Chequers early in July, and Churchill told him that he was expecting a majority of about a hundred. Then the day before the results were announced (26th July) he started to feel depressed, and at one moment he said that he was afraid of a stalemate. But in his blackest moment he had never anticipated anything like the landslide in favour of the Labour Party which actually occurred, and the figures were a bitter disappointment to him. As he himself put it later, "All our enemies having surrendered unconditionally or being about to do so, I was immediately dismissed by the British electorate from all further conduct of their affairs."

The final weekend in July 1945 was to be the last that Churchill would spend at Chequers for six years. By then he had already ceased to be Prime Minister, for he had resigned immediately it became clear that Labour had a majority. He drove down to Chequers on the afternoon of Saturday 28th July to collect his belongings and to say goodbye to the staff. It was lovely weather when he arrived there but he was feeling depressed. After dinner he and Mrs Churchill went up to the Long Gallery, where there was the usual film show. On this occasion it consisted of news reels of the Potsdam Conference, followed by an American documentary film entitled *The True Glory*. But this was soon over, and as Churchill made his way down to the Great Hall he remarked sadly "This is where I miss the news. . . . No work, nothing to do." In the past, once the cinema show was over, he had been accustomed to go down to the secretary's room, which led off from the Great Hall, there to read the latest messages which had come through from Whitehall; and frequently, last thing before retiring, he would ring the duty captain at the Admiralty and other duty officers to ask for the latest news. Now it was Attlee who was entitled to read the telegrams, while Churchill himself paced restlessly up and down the Great Hall. Commander Thompson tried to distract him by playing some of his favourite Gilbert and Sullivan records on

the gramophone, but this failed to cheer him up. Matters improved, however, when Thompson turned to martial music,
playing French and American military marches, and soon
Churchill was asking for some of his special favourites, "Run
Rabbit Run" and "The Wizard of Oz". By two o'clock in the
morning, at which hour he had decided to go to bed, he had
quite cheered up.

The next day some of his favourite visitors arrived. They
included 'The Prof' (Lord Cherwell), Brendan Bracken and
Winant. The Rector had been invited to tea, which was served
in the Great Hall. Churchill, who had spent the afternoon in bed,
was late for tea. He came down the stairs singing – completely
out of tune. Then he sat down at the tea table and, after muttering to himself for a few minutes, started to sing again, waving his
arms to and fro, as though beating time. At one point, he
suddenly broke off and looked across at the picture of "The Lion
and the Mouse" which occupies a prominent position in the
corner of the great hall. It was perhaps Churchill's favourite of
all the Chequers pictures, and he would often draw his guests'
attention to it. Indeed, he 'touched it up' with his own brush
and paint. On this occasion he said to the Rector, "You know
the Almighty should have left off when he created the animals.
He made a mistake in creating man." And when the Rector
spoke to him of the intelligence of his (Mr White's) dog,
Churchill said, "See that you put him on the voting list."

The weather had continued good, and after tea they all went
out into the garden, and Churchill sat down contentedly on a
seat in the corner of the lawn, watching some of his guests play
croquet. While this was happening, Randag, the tenant of the
home farm, arrived with his wife and some of his children to say
goodbye. These children had enjoyed many a Christmas party
at Chequers. Randag and his wife had a very large family, and
Churchill used to say that if you asked the Randag children you
had enough to make a party. On this occasion the Prime
Minister said to the Rector, pointing to them, "By the time
these children grow up we shall all be Socialists."

The next day, before leaving Chequers, each of the guests
signed the visitors' book. Churchill was the last to do so, and
after his name he added in capitals the one word, FINIS. A few

weeks later the Lees received the following letter from Mrs Churchill:

My dear Lord and Lady Lee

Our last weekend at Chequers was sad. But as we all wrote our names in the Visitors' Book I reflected upon the wonderful part this ancient house has played in the war. What distinguished guests it has sheltered, what momentous meetings it has witnessed, what fateful decisions have been taken under its roof.

Indeed, you were both inspired when you gave it to the Nation and how happy you must be that you gave this noble gift early in your lives; so that you have seen the good it has done, is doing and will continue to do.

Winston and I both thank you for the help and comfort it has been to him in these tremendous years.

Yours affectionately,

Clementine S. Churchill.

11

The Second Labour Prime Minister

THERE has been some speculation as to how Clement Attlee, who succeeded Churchill as Prime Minister in July 1945, managed to survive so successfully the strain of being Prime Minister for nearly six years, following on an important position and great responsibility in the wartime government with less than a week's holiday before he embarked on his new duties. Chequers had a great deal to do with it. He went there a lot and made full use of its amenities. In the summer he played a lot of tennis and croquet; indeed, he was certainly the most frequent and perhaps the only user of the tennis court at Chequers. He soon fell in love with the Buckinghamshire countryside, and so fond did he become of the district that when he ceased to be Prime Minister he acquired a country home of his own not very far from Chequers.

There have probably been other Prime Ministers who were as fond of or even fonder than Attlee was of Chequers, but it is perhaps true to say that there had never before been a Prime Minister's family as a whole which have loved the place and looked on it as their country home to the extent that the Attlees did. From the moment that they first entered the place, not only Attlee himself but his wife, son and three daughters took instinctively to Chequers. It was a unique experience for them because they had never had a country home of their own before. Attlee went there almost every weekend when the House was sitting and at holiday times as well. Indeed, in the summer he was sometimes there for several weeks at a stretch. His children were also thrilled by the place. One or more of his daughters was there most weekends, but his son, Martin, was in the Merchant

Navy and was not there quite so often. But Martin (the present Earl) will yield to no one in admiration of and affection for the place. Everything about it appealed to him. He particularly enjoyed going out with a gun in the company of chauffeurs and detectives to shoot rabbits and squirrels on the estate. The whole family (with the possible exception of Attlee himself) were convinced that there was a Chequers ghost.

Attlee never entertained on anything like the scale that Churchill did. But there was nearly always a weekend party there during the Attlee period, and the Prime Minister invited not only members of the Government but also distinguished statesmen from the Commonwealth and foreign countries. It was his opinion that the historical associations of Chequers made a distinct impression on those who came from 'younger countries'.

But it was not only politicians that he invited to visit him in Buckinghamshire. Many of his friends went there too and found it a delightful experience. For Attlee was an excellent host, and those who got to know him well soon realized that the common impression of him as dull and nondescript was entirely false. He was an excellent conversationalist, and his comments on men and affairs were always pithy and worth listening to. His conversation with his visitors at Chequers was never interlarded with fine phrases and rolling periods as Churchill's sometimes was. On the contrary, such expressions as "rotten", piffle", "tripe", "a good egg" often featured in his vocabulary when he was talking to his friends and acquaintances. Like Ramsay MacDonald, he never regarded the possession of Chequers as being in the least inconsistent with his Socialism. Both men would have disagreed completely with Lloyd George's point of view here.

Attlee had a strong sense of history, and Chequers' past associations therefore made a great appeal to him. But he was keen on the garden too, though, unlike Ramsay MacDonald and Neville Chamberlain, he did not do any significant amount of manual work outside himself. Once, when asked whether he was any good at gardening, he described himself as "a good rough weeder". Then he added "Look at the number of things in the bed, chuck out the majority. They'll be the weeds." Then, after a few puffs at his pipe, he went on, "One of the things I've learnt in politics."

Nothing like the number of high-ranking military men came to Chequers during Attlee's as during Churchill's premiership. Indeed, serving officers were the exception rather than the rule among the guests during this latter period. But just after Christmas 1947 Field Marshal Lord Alanbrooke, one of the most famous of them all, went there once again. The Attlees had just spent a very happy Christmas in the old house, and Christmas cards and decorations were very much in evidence. To the Field Marshal the whole atmosphere of the place was very different from what he last remembered. A flood of memories swept over him. It had been there in November 1941 that Churchill had invited him to undertake the tremendous responsibility of becoming C.I.G.S. Of the memories and the thoughts which Chequers evoked Brooke himself wrote:

> I remember the night Winston offered me the job of C.I.G.S. in the large smoking-room at Chequers, and when he went out of the room shortly afterwards I was so overcome that my natural impulse was, when left alone, to kneel and pray to God for his assistance in my new task. I have often looked back, during the last three and a half years, to that prayer. I am not a highly religious individual, according to many people's outlook. I am, however, convinced that there is a God, all-powerful, looking after the destiny of this world. I had little doubt about this before the war started, but this war has convinced me more than ever of this truth. Again and again during the last six years I have seen His hand guiding and controlling the destiny of this world towards that final and definite destiny which He has ordained.
>
> The suffering and agony of war must exist gradually to educate us up to the fundamental law of "loving our neighbour as ourselves". When this lesson has been learned, then war will cease to exist. We are, however, many centuries from such a state of affairs. Many more wars and much suffering is still required before we finally learn our lesson. Humanity on this world is, however, still young; there are many millions of years to run during which perfection will be attained. For the present we can do no more than go on striving to improve more friendly relations towards those that surround us.

The only two Prime Ministers to hold wedding receptions at Chequers were both Socialists. One of Attlee's daughters, like

one of Ramsay MacDonald's, married while her father was
Prime Minister, and in both cases full advantage was taken of
the delightful surroundings and other amenities which Chequers
had to offer. The wedding of Miss Janet Helen Attlee, the Prime
Minister's eldest daughter, to Mr H. W. Shipton took place at
Ellesborough parish church on 15th November 1947. After the
service the guests were conveyed by bus to Chequers, where
they were received by the Prime Minister and Mrs Attlee. The
party included Lord and Lady Jowitt, the Speaker of the House
of Commons and Mrs Clifton Brown, Sir Stafford and Lady
Cripps, and a past and two future occupants of the place, Mrs
Winston Churchill and Mr and Mrs Harold Wilson. The
presents, which were displayed in the Great Hall, included a
silver tea pot, milk jug and sugar basin from the King and
Queen, a dinner service from Queen Mary, a dressing table set
from members of the Cabinet, a china coffee set from the
Speaker and Mrs Clifton Brown and a silver casket from Mr and
Mrs Churchill.

Attlee managed to get through a lot of work while he was at
Chequers, but he was a very quick reader and extremely good at
getting a lot accomplished in a short time. The family generally
arrived on Friday evening and left on Monday morning. Attlee
brought a great sheaf of Cabinet and other papers with him
when he arrived, and a fresh batch almost invariably came from
Whitehall on the Saturday morning. Breakfast was always early,
and he would work steadily in his study until lunch time, by which
time he had generally got through the work and he could and
did devote the rest of the day to relaxation and pleasure. In the
afternoon he would either go for a walk, play golf or (in the
summer) play tennis with his family, visitors or local friends. In
the evening he would either read, play games with his family or
watch a film. The cinema apparatus set up by Churchill in the
Long Gallery was still there when Attlee arrived, though it was
later removed by the Ministry of Works, who considered it to be
a fire hazard.

Evening dress was always worn for dinner during the time
that Attlee was at Chequers.

Christmas was a great time at Chequers during the Attlee
period. The whole family felt that they had received so much

from Chequers that they must do what they could to give something back, and Christmas seemed a particularly appropriate time at which to do so. There was always one meal during the festive season at which the family (Attlee included) waited on the staff. The practice of having a children's party on Boxing Day was continued. The Randags were always asked, but there were also the children of junior ministers and civil servants. Attlee joined in the games, and as they were leaving he said goodbye to and shook hands with each of his guests in turn – and knew nearly all the children's names.

Meanwhile, Miss Lamont had decided to retire and, largely as a result of a strong recommendation from Mrs Churchill, Mrs Hill, who had been Churchill's private secretary, was appointed curator. She remained for about twenty-four years, giving outstanding service, and on her retirement in 1969 she was presented with a silver salver inscribed with the signatures of all the Prime Ministers (including Churchill) for whom she had worked.

Among the members of his government whom Attlee invited to Chequers was Hugh Dalton who thought it was "rather overpowering" and "like living in a museum". He was critical of the Great Hall and thought it was cold and draughty.

In October 1951, there was a general election which the Labour Party lost.

12

The Return of
the Conservatives

WINSTON CHURCHILL now found himself Prime Minister for the second time. The intervening years had been busy and, on the whole, happy ones, though he had deplored the turning of the country by the Socialists into what he described as "one vast Wormwoodscrubbery". It has been suggested that he did not make as much use of Chequers in his second premiership as he did in his first, only going there when Mrs Churchill insisted that he should do so because of the heavy strain on the staff at Chartwell which large-scale entertainment there involved. A scrutiny of the visitors' book, however, makes it clear that he used Chequers a good deal during this period. He went there for the weekend soon after becoming Prime Minister for the second time, namely on 25th November 1951, and his visitors on this occasion included the Caseys and Lord Cherwell. He spent each of the next four Christmases at Chequers when the old house was given over to children's fun and laughter as seldom, if ever, before or since. For now there were not only his own grandchildren but also the Marlborough children who came over from Blenheim. The place was full to capacity so that even the small attics at the top of the house had to be turned out and used as bedrooms. And on Boxing Day there was the usual children's party.

Churchill was not at Chequers a great deal during the early part of 1953. He tended to go more to Chartwell at weekends. But by the summer Mrs Churchill had decided that weekend entertaining on the scale on which Churchill carried it out while Prime Minister imposed too great a strain on the staff at Chartwell, and certainly on this occasion it was she who insisted on a move to Chequers. They arrived there on 24th July and stayed continuously until 12th August, the longest time that Churchill was ever there at a stretch. The only other Prime Minister who has been there for a longer continuous period was Attlee, who would sometimes stay for several weeks on end during the summer.

Churchill had had a stroke on 24th June, and grave fears had been entertained about him, but his health improved rapidly after he got to Chequers. Arriving there on 27th July, Lord Moran found him "full of vigour and talk". His visitors during this period included Adlai Stevenson (whom he liked), Butler, Salisbury, Maxwell Fyffe, Leathers, Moir (his Solicitor) and Montgomery. On 8th August he presided over a meeting at Chequers to discuss the Soviet reply to a three-power note. He was in excellent and vigorous form and proposed action entirely contrary to that advocated by the Foreign Office. After lunch he drank brandy for the first time since his stroke and said that all his life he had found that his main contribution was by self expression rather than by self denial. During this time at Chequers he played croquet now and again in the afternoon, and this sometimes worried his nurse because he was apt to hurry after the ball and then become extremely short of breath. On 12th August he returned to London and from there went on to Chartwell. He returned to Chequers, however, towards the end of the month and stayed there for about ten days, during which time he did a certain amount of painting.

It was in August that Montgomery, by now a close friend of Churchill's, went to stay at Chequers for the weekend. On the Sunday he accompanied Mrs Churchill and other members of the family and house party to Ellesborough church. The Prime Minister, however, was not amongst those who went. The Rector invited the Field Marshal to read the lessons, and Montgomery did so, prefacing each lesson with a few introductory remarks of his own. After the service was over, Mrs Churchill invited the Rector to come back and have lunch at Chequers. In the course of the meal, one of the other guests congratulated Montgomery on the excellence of his introductory remarks in church. The Field Marshal was about to reply when he was interrupted by the Prime Minister. "You have no right to add to

Holy Writ," he said. "I did not add to Holy Writ," replied the Field Marshal, "I merely made a few introductory remarks." He then proceeded to repeat them, but the Prime Minister was not satisfied. "You *did* add to Holy Writ if you said all that," he remarked. "Why did you allow it, Rector?" Then he continued, addressing Montgomery, "What you should have done was to stand up and read what was in front of you like this, 'Here beginneth the so and so verse' of the whatever chapter it is of the particular book in the Bible you are reading from and speak out loudly and clearly." At this point, the Rector rather boldly intervened, "I suggest that the Prime Minister comes to church next Sunday and shows us how the lessons should be read himself, Field Marshal," he said.

"Does he read the lessons?" enquired Montgomery.

"Not as yet," said the Rector. "He has said on at least one occasion that he would, then he wouldn't, then he would but in the end he didn't."

"Does he come to church at all?" asked the Field Marshal.

"Ah! he often embarrasses me in that respect," said the Rector.

"Embarrass you? How do I embarrass you?" asked Churchill. "What do you mean?"

"Well, people often ask me whether the Prime Minister is a churchman."

"What do you tell them?" asked the Prime Minister, at the same time nudging the Rector with his elbow.

"I tell them one could hardly refer to him as a churchman but I think that at the very bottom of him he is a Christian."

"Tell them that I am an episcopalian," said Churchill.

During Churchill's second premiership Attlee and Mrs Attlee were his guests at Chequers on no less than four occasions. Few men have loathed Socialism more wholeheartedly than did Churchill but there were individual Socialists that he liked and Attlee was one of them. So was Ernest Bevin, whose widow Churchill also invited to Chequers.

After Churchill had resigned in April 1955, he gave a farewell party at 10 Downing Street to which all the staff both there and at Chequers were invited. Each of them received a present. Having spent the weekend there, he signed the Chequers

visitors' book for the last time on 6th April 1955 and never went
back there again. But Lady Churchill was to return some ten
years later. The purpose of her visit was to meet the secretary to
the trustees and agree with him on the form which their
acknowledgement of the gift of the avenue of beech trees should
take. An inscription contained in an attractive gilt frame was
decided on, and this now hangs inside the front entrance porch.
The words are as follows: "The avenue of beech trees flanking
the Victory Drive was the gift of Sir Winston and Lady
Churchill in memory of the momentous days they spent at
Chequers from 1940–1945 and 1951–1955."

Churchill was succeeded as Prime Minister by Eden, who
spent the Easter holiday of 1955 at Chequers, to which he was
no newcomer. His first visit had been paid as long ago as 1926,
when Baldwin was the Prime Minister, and since then he had
been there frequently as the guest of Baldwin's various successors.
His association with the place thus went back for thirty years and
some of the most significant and dramatic scenes in his political
career had been enacted there. It was to Chequers that he went
in 1936 to discuss with Baldwin Hitler's reoccupation of the
Rhineland; it was at Chequers that he had his interview with
Neville Chamberlain over what Eden regarded as the latter's
"cold shouldering" of Roosevelt. It was at Chequers in June
1941 that he received the summons to the Prime Minister's
bedroom on the occasion of Hitler's attack on Russia. Indeed it
is probably true to say that no other Prime Minister has had a
longer or more continuous association with the place than he.

In April 1956 Chequers was again visited by an important
Russian delegation. This time the visitors were Bulganin and
Kruschev, but there were no such remarkable incidents as those
which occurred when Molotov came during the war as the guest
of Churchill. On the contrary, Eden found them "easy and
interesting to entertain". Gaitskell (then Leader of the Opposition) was invited to Chequers to meet them. He and Eden got on
quite well together, and even at the height of the Suez crisis, when
some of the angriest scenes of the century occurred in the House
of Commons, there was no real animosity between these two.

Lee had expressed the hope that Chequers and the pure air of
the Chilterns would act as "an anodyne" for the successive

Prime Ministers who went there. So far as Eden is concerned, these hopes can hardly be said to have been realized. As time went on stresses and strain became increasingly his lot, mounting to a crescendo during the Suez crisis in the autumn of 1956. During this period, he would arrive back at Chequers utterly worn out after an extremely exhausting week, during which, from time to time, he had been bawled at and yelled at in the House of Commons; but, though he had shown signs of the colossal strain, he had remained invariably courteous and, as one Labour member put it, however much you might disagree with him "you couldn't but admire the cold courage of the man". Because of the differences in time, news was liable to come at almost any hour of the day or night from the United Nations headquarters in New York, from the Middle East or from Whitehall. No day and no hour was sacrosanct, and an immediate and worrying decision was just as likely to have to be taken on a Sunday at Chequers as on a weekday in Downing Street.

The second weekend in October 1956 was a particularly tiring but on the whole a heartening one for Eden. On the Saturday, 14th October, he had travelled down to Llandudno to deliver his address on the last day of the Conservative Conference. He had been loudly cheered before beginning, at the end of and at intervals during his speech, in the course of which he said: "Through all these negotiations, peace has been our aim, but not peace at any price – because in dealing with a dictatorship peace at any price means to increase step by step the danger of universal war. What is at stake is not just the canal, important though that is. It is the sanctity of international engagements. This is the supreme lesson of the period between the wars. . . ."

The following day (Sunday) Eden was at Chequers for an important meeting with the French. With Eden was Anthony Nutting, Minister of State at the Foreign Office, who has given the following account of what took place. According to him:

> Challe then proceeded to outline what he termed a possible plan of action for Britain and France to gain physical control of the Suez Canal. The plan was that Israel should be invited to attack Egypt across the Sinai Peninsula and that France and Britain

having given the Israeli forces enough time to seize all or most of
Sinai should then order both sides to withdraw . . . in order to
permit an Anglo-French force to intervene and occupy the Canal
on the pretext of saving it from damage. . . .

Christmas 1956 was rather a sad one at Chequers, for Eden's
health had been undermined by the prolonged strain of the
Suez crisis and he now realized that it was unlikely that he could
remain Prime Minister much longer. On Boxing Day there was
a large lunch party; the guests included Lords Kilmuir and
Salisbury as well as R. A. Butler, Lennox Boyd, Gwilym Lloyd
George and Anthony Head. Before lunch the Ministers had a
long discussion about the clearance of the Suez Canal and
drafted a message on this subject to the British representative at
the United Nations headquarters in New York. The result of
this was that it was not until about 2.15 p.m. that the party sat
down in the dining room for lunch.

Eden asked Kilmuir to stay behind after the others had left,
and he took him into the White Parlour. Many consider this
room, with its white panelling, Hepplewhite chairs and the six
small Constable pictures on the walls, to be the most attractive
room at Chequers, and on this occasion it was looking particularly nice because of the large number of Christmas cards and
the charming and tasteful manner in which Lady Eden had
arranged them. Eden asked Kilmuir, as an old friend, for his
advice as to whether he should stay on. The doubt in Eden's
mind was whether, in view of the deterioration in his health, he
was justified in carrying on. Kilmuir advised him strongly to do
so, reminding him of "the deeply rooted loyalty of the Conservative Party" and of the amount of support and goodwill
towards him which undoubtedly existed in the country. But
these arguments did not have any appreciable effect on the
course of events. At a Cabinet meeting held early in the New
Year Eden announced his intention of resigning. He paid his
last visit to Chequers a day or two later – early in January 1957.
It was then that M. Spaak, Belgian Foreign Minister, came to
see him. They were old friends, having been associated in the
foreign affairs of their two countries for more than twenty years.
Spaak was the last European statesman to be entertained by
Eden at Chequers.

During their time at Chequers Lady Eden took a great interest in the garden and did a lot to improve it.

Harold Macmillan, who followed Anthony Eden as Prime Minister, was not one of those who have used it most or who have derived the greatest benefit from it. One of the reasons for this was that, like Churchill, he had a house of his own, Birch Grove in Sussex, to which he was already deeply attached. During a considerable part of his premiership, he handed over the use and occupation of Chequers to the Chancellor of the Exchequer, Selwyn Lloyd. During these years, however, two extremely important foreign visitors came to England and both were entertained at Chequers by the Prime Minister himself. They were Conrad Adenauer, Chancellor of West Germany, and Dwight D. Eisenhower, thirty-second President of the United States.

When Eisenhower arrived at Chequers on 29th August 1959 for his two-day visit with Harold Macmillan, it was rather over fifteen years since he had last been there – in July 1944, when he was the Supreme Commander of the Allied Forces in Europe. He was now more than half-way through his second term as President of the United States. It had saddened him, as he had told Churchill in a letter, that over Suez, "I and my old friends of years have met a problem concerning which we do not see eye to eye." He had added that "I shall never be happy until our old-time closeness has been restored."

It was equally the wish both of the British people and of Eisenhower's host at Chequers that "the old time closeness should be restored". As to the public, the warmth of the reception accorded to the President wherever he went in Britain, including the approaches to Chequers, was clear evidence of this fact, while from the moment that he was greeted by Macmillan a most cordial atmosphere prevailed. The two men had known each other well during the war. They had met for the first time in Algiers in 1943 when Eisenhower was the Commander-in-Chief of the Allied Forces in that theatre and Macmillan was the British Political Adviser. From the start they had got on well, and they continued to do so on this occasion.

Seldom if ever before had Chequers received such attention from the Press. Some 400 journalists invaded the neighbour-

hood, but about all they learnt was that Eisenhower slept in a
'four-poster' bed and that the Queen had sent six brace of young
grouse to Chequers as a gift to the President. Eisenhower gave
the following account of the visit in his memoirs:

> We wasted little time in getting down to business. With lunch at
> 2 p.m., Harold and I met with our advisers immediately after-
> wards in a spacious room on the second floor. As always, the dis-
> cussion was wide ranging. . . . The first meeting over, we took our
> golf clubs to the surrounding green gardens and set about devising
> a makeshift golf game. Surrounding the house at Chequers is a
> stone wall several feet high and beyond this, on one side, is a
> sizeable field. We placed a golf bag at the foot of the wall as a
> target and, by going to the far end of the field, were able to set up
> a shot of something over 150 yards. This provided a competitive
> setting and we played the British against the Americans – Harold
> Macmillan and Selwyn Lloyd against Jock Whitney and me.
> With each side given an equal number of shots, we tried to hit the
> bag more often than they did, but at the end of two rounds all was
> well for both sides. The British won the first round five to four and
> the Americans the second four to three. This was a good point at
> which to quit and so we went back to get ready for the evening.
> . . . At 7 p.m. Harold and I met with only our two foreign
> ministers present. . . .
> The next morning, Sunday, the four of us again conferred.
> Following this conversation we attended church. The Ellesborough
> church is a quaint structure; on this occasion its quaintness was
> strained by overcrowding. I was offered the privilege of reading the
> daily lesson but felt it proper to decline in favour of my host.
> Accordingly, Harold did so himself, as apparently was his habit
> whenever he went to Chequers.

The occasion just referred to had aroused widespread interest
and was certainly unique – the only one on which President and
Prime Minister have worshipped together in an English country
church, though Roosevelt and Churchill attended divine
service together on board a British battleship and again at
Richmond in Virginia, and in December 1918 Woodrow Wilson
had made his famous 'journey of the heart' to the chapel in
Carlisle where his mother had worshipped and of which his
father had been the minister.

Both Eisenhower and Macmillan were deeply religious men.
At his inauguration ceremony, standing on a raised dais at the

East Front of the Capitol and facing the enormous crowd below, Eisenhower had started his address with a prayer. Now he found himself in a very different atmosphere. But as he and Macmillan knelt in quiet prayer in this beautiful little church in the heart of Buckinghamshire they were both deeply conscious of the source from which all true wisdom proceeds. The Rector received appreciative letters from them both about the service. Macmillan wrote:

> I would like you to know how moved the President and I were by the church service this morning. It cannot be easy for a church in a rural parish to have to include amongst the congregation people in the public eye whose presence is likely to attract great crowds. There must also be a temptation perhaps to do rather more than is usual. But the arrangements in the church were very dignified and simple and you conducted the service in such a way as to let the quiet rhythm of the Anglican order of prayer convey its message.
>
> Yours very sincerely,
Harold Macmillan.

Before leaving Chequers, Eisenhower planted a tree in the grounds to commemorate his visit. It was a rare and interesting specimen known as a Dawn Redwood.

The other important visitor whom Macmillan entertained at Chequers was the octogenarian Chancellor of West Germany – Conrad Adenauer, mayor of Cologne from 1917 to 1933, in which latter year he was summarily dismissed by the Nazis, by whom he was also sentenced later to two short terms of imprisonment. In June 1945 he was reinstated by the American military government as mayor; but the following October the government of the city was transferred to the British, who promptly dismissed Adenauer on the ground apparently that he had displayed "insufficient energy in preparing for emergency dwellings in winter". His second wife had been ill in Cologne at the time and military regulations did not permit him, as a deposed mayor, to go into the city to see her. He had undoubtedly felt this keenly at the time.

Now everything possible was being done to give him a warm welcome and assurances of British goodwill, and in this Chequers played an important part, for Macmillan took the unusual step of inviting him down there in the middle of the week. The Prime Minister and German Chancellor arrived there on the afternoon of Wednesday 18th November 1959, and they both stayed the night. They had their first series of talks that evening and these lasted for about four hours. They had more talks the next morning for two hours. Then they had lunch, at which meal Anthony Eden was amongst the guests. He had come over specially. Before leaving, Adenauer was shown all over Chequers and he evinced keen interest (amongst other things) in the pictures, particularly the Rembrandts.

Between 1957 and 1962 the Minister who used Chequers most frequently was probably Selwyn Lloyd. When he first went there, he was Foreign Secretary and he is probably the last holder of that office who will use Chequers because the modern practice is for the Foreign Secretary to use Dorneywood, also in Buckinghamshire (near Burnham Beeches), as his country residence. Dorneywood had been given to the National Trust in 1942 by the late Lord Courtauld-Thompson to be used after his death (which occurred in 1954) as a residence for the Prime Minister or other senior Minister nominated by him. In June 1955 the then Prime Minister (Anthony Eden), nominated the then Secretary of State for Commonwealth Relations (Lord Home) as the first official resident of Dorneywood. When in 1960 he succeeded Selwyn Lloyd as Foreign Secretary Lord Home (as he then was) continued as official resident of Dorneywood and Selwyn Lloyd continued to use Chequers until he ceased to be a Minister in July 1962.

One of the practical results of this arrangement from Selwyn Lloyd's point of view was that as he was not the official occupant he was not entitled to the allowance which that occupant received when in residence. But this was a small matter in comparison with the enormous boon which he found Chequers to be and the great enjoyment and benefit which he derived through being there. His favourite recreations at Chequers were playing golf, going for long walks and, in the summer, playing croquet on the lawn. He had a small daughter who revelled in the place and soon became a great favourite. Though not himself an Anglican, he went regularly to Ellesborough Church on Sundays and read the lessons. He took a

Winston Churchill after the outbreak of war with Japan in 1941

(*left*) Harold Macmillan and President Eisenhower in the grounds of Chequers, August 1949. (*below*) Macmillan with rival test captains, Frank Worrell of the West Indies and Ted Dexter of England, two of the many guests entertained at Chequers

keen interest in the whole place and was for a time the chairman of the trustees. He was very good about keeping in touch with Lady Lee, writing to her and going to see her and telling her about Chequers and how much he liked the place, and she greatly appreciated this. While Chancellor of the Exchequer, he spent the weekends preceding each of his two budgets at Chequers, and it was there that he completed the preparation of his budget speeches.

During the latter part of his premiership, Macmillan went to Chequers a good deal more than he did during the earlier part. His wife took a particularly keen interest in the garden and made many constructive suggestions. Macmillan's own special delight was the library. Certainly, amongst the post-war Prime Ministers none has made fuller use of this than did Macmillan. Most of the books are contained in shelves which run the full length of the Long Gallery, to which Macmillan would repair after dinner and where he would remain until far into the night. There are over 5,000 volumes at Chequers, and many Greek and Latin classics are included; Macmillan, a fine scholar, was particularly interested in these. There is also a fine collection of French literature of the eighteenth century, with good illustrations and choice bindings, and there are a number of rare and valuable books of an earlier date than this. The original collection was curiously deficient in nineteenth-century literature but the Lees did a good deal to repair this, leaving behind a large number of the Victorian classics (including several first editions), beautifully bound, from their own collections. Most of the books in the Long Gallery, however, are of the sixteenth, seventeenth and eighteenth centuries, and many are in their original bindings with their owner's autographs or book plates in them. To Macmillan, with his great knowledge of books, all this was fascinating. Ramsay MacDonald was also very keen on the library and spent £40 out of his own pocket in having certain of the volumes rebound.

In the autumn of 1963, Chequers was subjected rather unexpectedly to a change of tenancy. For some time past there had been discontent among a certain highly vocal section of the Conservative Party, both inside and outside the House of Commons, with the leadership of Macmillan. This section was

L

probably not very strong numerically and there is no particular reason to suppose that Macmillan himself was either worried by or inclined to take any special notice of them. Indeed it is fairly certain that, until he was taken ill, he had every intention of carrying on. There was a family party at Chequers in October 1963, and the general feeling, which Macmillan shared, was that he should lead the party into battle at the next election; but shortly after this he had to go into hospital for an operation, and his doctors advised him that he would need a considerable period of complete rest. In these circumstances, he decided to resign from the leadership of the Conservative Party and from the office of Prime Minister.

It so happened that at the moment that Macmillan reached this decision the Conservative Party Conference was being held at Blackpool. The letter in which he had made clear his intentions was read out to the delegates in the middle of the proceedings, and, with the leadership issue thus thrown wide open, the atmosphere in Blackpool was more like an American convention than a normal party conference. There was even a "smoke-filled room". The British counterpart of Colonel Harvey's suite at the Blackstone Hotel, Chicago was Lord Dilhorne's bedroom at the Imperial Hotel, Blackpool. Into this room each member of the Cabinet went to give his opinion about who should be the new leader. In due course, after these and other "normal processes of discussion" had taken place, the Queen sent for Lord Home, then Foreign Secretary, and asked him to form a Government. Later, having become Prime Minister, he resigned his peerage and became a member of the House of Commons and leader of the Conservative Party.

Sir Alec Douglas Home was no stranger to Buckinghamshire when he arrived at Chequers; for the past eight years he had been the official occupant of nearby Dorneywood. He is the only Prime Minister who, so far, has been the official occupant of each of these two houses in turn. Apart from Bonar Law, who never occupied it at all, Sir Alec's tenure of Chequers was shorter than that of any of the other Prime Ministers. But he and his wife became extremely fond of both the house and the garden. Sir Alec's favourite room was the White Parlour. He was not alone in this preference.

Like Churchill and Macmillan, Sir Alec owned a large country house during the whole of the time he was at Chequers, and he liked to spend as much of his holidays as he could there. But, unlike those of the other two, his was an ancestral mansion which his family had owned for generations. Before he resigned his peerage, he had been the fourteenth Earl of Home – a fact which was often referred to during this period and sometimes in a disparaging sense.

"The message that has gone out to the world," declared Harold Wilson, "is that in 1963 the Government party selects its leaders and the country's Prime Minister through the machinery of an aristocratic cabal. In this ruthlessly competitive, scientific, technical, industrial age, a week of intrigues has produced a result based on family and hereditary connections. The leader has emerged – an elegant anachronism."

But this particular tirade recoiled upon the head of its author. Thus "A Socialist Housewife" wrote to *The Times* that she would vote Conservative at the next election as a protest against "Mr. Wilson's public rudeness to a gentleman of such obvious breeding" as Home. And Sir Alec himself managed to turn the sneers about the 'Fourteenth Earl' to good account. "As far as 'the fourteenth earl' is concerned," he said on television, "I suppose Mr Wilson when you come to think of it is the fourteenth Mr Wilson. I don't really see why criticism should centre on this. If all men are equal – well that's a very good doctrine. But are we to say that all men are equal except peers? And nobody can be Prime Minister because he happens to be an earl?"

13

The Third Labour Prime Minister and the Thirty-seventh President

NINE months later, there was a General Election which the Conservatives lost, and Sir Alec accordingly resigned.

Sir Alec's successor as Prime Minister was Harold Wilson, who thus became the third Labour leader to occupy Chequers. Like his two predecessors, he has made good use of the place, using it most weekends and going there also from time to time for short holiday breaks at Christmas, Easter and in the summer. He has instituted the excellent practice of signing the visitors' book himself on at least most of the occasions that he goes there, and this, from the point of view of the historical writer, is most helpful. His predecessors have in general only signed it on the occasion of their first and last visits. Wilson's first weekend there as Prime Minister was that of 20th to 22nd November, and his guests included Patrick Gordon Walker, Arthur Bottomley, Roy Jenkins and James Callaghan. In contrast with Ramsay MacDonald he has from time to time entertained and had discussions with all his Cabinet colleagues at Chequers. Others whose names appear in the visitors' book during Wilson's premiership include Earl Mountbatten, Earl Attlee, Lord Thomson of Fleet, Mr Kosygin (Prime Minister of Russia), who was there in February 1967, and Hubert Humphrey, Vice-President of the United States, who was a weekend guest there early the following April. President Nixon's visit will be referred to later.

During recent years Chequers has tended to be used more and

more for large-scale conferences, and this is a tendency which has been accentuated since Harold Wilson became Prime Minister. Other Prime Ministers have tended to hold the larger meetings and formal conferences at Downing Street, reserving Chequers for smaller and more intimate gatherings at the weekends. Harold Wilson, however, has tended to hold rather bigger conferences and meetings at Chequers during his weekends there than did his predecessors. On more than one occasion he has presided over a full meeting of the Cabinet at Chequers. There was a large Ministerial and party conference at Chequers in February 1946, and in June 1967 the National Executive Committee of the Labour Party met there, when most members of the Cabinet attended. In all some forty-six people were present at this latter meeting – probably the largest ever to be held at Chequers. These meetings are normally held in the large room on the first floor which used to be called the great parlour but is now called the conference room.

There have also been a number of important overseas visitors to Chequers during Wilson's premiership. Some of the E.F.T.A. Ministers dined there early in December 1966 and Wilson arrived back from his encounter with Ian Smith on H.M.S. *Tiger* just in time to greet them. And in January 1967 the then Chancellor of the Exchequer (James Callaghan) met and entertained there the Finance Ministers of the United States, France, West Germany and Italy, with a view to exploring the possibility of an all-round reduction in interest rates. They all spent the Saturday night at Chequers and had their first meeting, which lasted three hours, that evening. They had another meeting of about the same duration the next day and this was followed by lunch. The *communiqué* which was prepared afterwards announced that "The Ministers agreed that they would all make it their object within the limits of their respective responsibilities to co-operate in administrative matters." Interest rates have risen almost continuously ever since.

Harold Wilson is extremely industrious, and his work normally continues throughout his weekends at Chequers, though he does from time to time manage to get in a game of golf on the Ellesborough course. The Prime Minister of the day is invariably made an honorary member of this club, and Wilson is one of the

Prime Ministers to make most use of this facility. Lloyd George also played there occasionally. Churchill never did, but he sometimes got one of his secretaries to ring up the club to arrange for one of his guests who was staying at Chequers to have a game.

Wilson has continued the practice followed by his predecessors of exploiting the amenities of Chequers to the full for the entertainment of delegates to the Prime Ministers' Conference. In the past the Prime Minister of the day has sometimes delegated this duty to one of his senior colleagues, but Wilson has invariably entertained them there himself. There have been sixteen of these conferences since 1944, and at all of them some of the Prime Ministers and Presidents of the Commonwealth countries have been entertained at Chequers. This has been increasingly the case in recent years as the following particulars show. At the 1955 meeting eight Prime Ministers were entertained at Chequers, at the 1956 meeting five, at the 1960 meeting one President and seven Prime Ministers. The figures for 1961, 1964, 1965 and 1966 were two Presidents, seven Prime Ministers; three Presidents, twelve Prime Ministers; four Presidents, eleven Prime Ministers; and one President, nine Prime Ministers respectively. In addition other Commonwealth representatives have generally also been included in the invitations to Chequers on the occasion of these meetings. Furthermore, in between the official conferences and meetings, Commonwealth Prime Ministers who happened to be in England have been invited to Chequers by the British Prime Minister of the day. Thus Nehru and Mrs Pandit were the guests of Anthony Eden at Chequers when the latter was there over Christmas 1956.

In connection with the 1969 Prime Ministers' Conference, Chequers and Dorneywood were both particularly well to the fore. On Friday 10th January the Prime Minister entertained ten Commonwealth guests to dinner at Chequers, including Presidents Nyerere and Kaunda (Tanzania and Zambia respectively) and the Prime Ministers of Canada, Malta and Botswana. His guests for dinner the next evening included Archbishop Makarios (President of the Republic of Cyprus) and the Prime Ministers of Australia, Gambia, Guyana, Lesotho and Barbados. The Prime Minister of Australia and his wife had lunch at Chequers on the Sunday, while that evening Wilson entertained there to dinner twelve Commonwealth guests, including the President of Uganda and the Prime Ministers of New Zealand, Malaysia, Trinidad and Tobago, Ceylon, Mauritius, Sierra Leone and Swaziland. Furthermore most of these Presidents and Prime Ministers were also entertained at Dorneywood by the Foreign Secretary during the same weekend.

By far the most important visitor to Chequers during Wilson's time there was Richard Nixon, thirty-seventh President of the United States, who was there for dinner on the evening of Monday 24th February 1969. It had been originally intended that he and Wilson should fly from London airport to Chequers in a United States government helicopter, but the weather proved too bad for this, so they drove out by car. It took them nearly an hour and a half, and this gave them time for a preliminary talk.

This was Nixon's first visit to Chequers, but the name was familiar to him for he had a dog called Checkers which figured prominently in a famous broadcast which he made at a crucial moment in his career. In the course of his campaign for the Vice-Presidency in 1952, Nixon had been attacked for receiving financial support from certain rich men and financial interests in California and elsewhere. Defending himself, he had given a full account of his financial position and then said, "Well that's about it. That's what we have and that's what we owe. It isn't very much but Pat and I have the satisfaction that every dime that we've got is honestly ours. I should say this – that Pat doesn't have a mink coat. But she does have a respectable Republican cloth coat. And I always tell her that she'd look good in anything. One other thing I should tell you . . . we did get a gift . . . a little cocker spaniel dog . . . and our little girl – Tricia, the 6 year old – named it Checkers. And you know the kids love that dog and I want to say this right now, that regardless of what they say about it we're going to keep it. . . ."

The broadcast was a great success. When, the following evening, the aeroplane carrying Nixon and his party landed at Wheeling, Virginia, Eisenhower was there with outstretched arms to greet him, and when Nixon said to the Presidential Candidate, "What are you doing here, General? You didn't have to come here to meet us," Eisenhower put his arm around him and replied, "I certainly did, Dick. You're my boy." After this Checkers became almost as famous as Roosevelt's dog, Fala, for a similar reason, and 'The Checkers Speech' became part of the political vocabulary of America. A new social organization, 'The Order of the Hound's Tooth' was founded, and the membership card, designed by Nixon himself, contained a portrait of Checkers.

We must now turn from the dog called Checkers to describe what happened at the house called Chequers when the President and the Prime Minister arrived there. Some fifteen journalists (eight British and seven American) managed to get into the house. Photographs were taken of the President and the Prime Minister in the Great Hall and the Long Gallery, and some of these pictures appeared on television. It was about seven p.m. when the two statesmen arrived at Chequers, and before dinner they talked together alone in the Long Gallery.

The Prime Minister's guests at dinner were, on the American side, the President, the Secretary of State, Doctor Kissinger, and the American ambassador, and on the British side the Foreign Secretary, the Secretary of the Cabinet, the Head of the Diplomatic Service and two of the Prime Minister's private secretaries. The menu was consommé soup, roast duck with apple sauce, orange slices and vegetables; norwegian cream and coffee. There was also a buffet supper served in the Hawtrey Room for other British and American guests.

After dinner the talks were resumed in the Long Gallery, but on this occasion other Ministers and officials were present. The talks ranged widely over world problems. The President did not spend the night at Chequers but left at about 11 p.m. and drove to London, where he had a suite reserved for him at Claridges hotel.

14

The Chequers Estate

WHEN Lee handed over Chequers to the nation the area which he had in hand and was farming himself was about 700 acres. This, at first, he retained, including only the house and its immediate surroundings – about 500 acres – in his original gift. The part which he kept had been up till then, and continued for a short time thereafter, to be farmed by his able baliff, Angus Chisholm. It was not long, however, before Lee decided that it was a mistake for the estate to be divided into two, and in May 1921 he wrote to the Minister of Agriculture, telling him that he had decided to relinquish in favour of the Ministry the land hitherto retained. The Minister, Sir Arthur Griffiths Boscawen, replied, thanking him and adding:

It is proposed that the main farm should be conducted as an example of a stock rearing farm, showing how land of that character could be improved so as to produce the maximum output of live stock consistent with sound commercial agriculture. It is my opinion that the farm could be made a valuable demonstration of the growth of improved varieties of cereals and fodder crops and of the amelioration of grass land, to be utilised for the intensive breeding and rearing of live stock, without departing from the prime economic purpose of any farm which is intended to guide the practice of the working farmer. At the same time it is hoped to come to some arrangement with the Bucks County Council under which the Dropshort Farm could be utilised for more definitely educational purposes as the holding attached to a Farm Institute. Thinking as I do that the future of agriculture in this country mainly depends upon the development of education and the spread of information among the farming community, it would give me the greatest satisfaction to know that for all time the Prime Minister of the day would be able to see at his doors an example of agricultural education in being. I hope to provide you very shortly with a more elaborate plan for the management of the farms. Meantime, in accepting your gift on behalf of the Ministry, I should wish to express my personal pleasure in being associated with the inception of a scheme so wisely and munificently conceived in the interests of agriculture by one who has already done so much for those interests.

Yours sincerely,

Arthur G. Boscawen.

But the high hopes expressed in these letters were not realized. Farming from Whitehall did not prove to be a great success, and Lee urged upon the trustees that the farms should be handed over to them as part of the permanent endowment. This having been done, the farm lands were let, and Angus Chisholm, the former bailiff, became the tenant and remained so until about 1935, when he was succeeded by the present tenant, Mr Eugene Randag.

Meanwhile, considerable changes have taken place in the method of financing the upkeep of Chequers – outside as well as inside. In making the original endowment, Lee had stipulated that, out of the income, £500 per annum should be spent on gardeners' wages, that the wages of four indoor servants should be paid out of it, that the Prime Minister or other official occupant should receive £15 for any continuous period of not less than thirty-six hours that he spent there and that the residue should be spent on internal and external maintenance. Most of the capital was invested in war loan and other fixed interest securities, and in due course the income became eroded by inflation. Even in the time of Neville Chamberlain things were getting difficult, and Chamberlain, who was not a wealthy man, complained that he was unable to keep the place up as he would have liked without dipping into his private resources.

Matters came to a head with the advent to power of Labour in 1945 and the arrival of Attlee at Chequers. By then the cost of living had risen steeply, and the endowment provided by Lee was nothing like sufficient. An expert on country houses, called in by the trustees, had reported in 1945 that "The existing garden staff is wholly inadequate to maintain the gardens in their proper state. . . . In my opinion the minimum staff requisite to maintain the gardens would be the head gardener

and three men under him." In fact, at that time one old man was
trying to do the whole thing himself, with a little casual help in
the summer. Shortly after the war Sir Stafford Cripps expressed
the view that, unless a great deal of money was spent on the
place, it would become like "a derelict Irish farm" and that it
should either have the requisite amount of money spent on it or
be given up.

At a meeting of the trustees held in March 1949, Cripps, then
Chancellor of the Exchequer, again stressed the financial
problems facing the trustees and outlined various possible
solutions. The Prime Minister (Attlee) said that on no account
must anything be done which would be contrary to the wishes
of the donors, but, upon the assumption that they would be
agreeable, he suggested, and the meeting ultimately agreed, that
the Ministry of Works should take over all the land and
buildings, be entitled to receive the farm rents and be responsible for internal as well as structural maintenance of the
house, leaving the trustees only in charge of domestic arrangements. The Lees were consulted and were agreeable, as also
was the Leader of the Opposition, Churchill.

The new arrangement was implemented, but it did not work
well. The duality of control as between the trustees and the
Ministry was found to lead to difficulties. Furthermore, owing to
continued inflation, the income from the endowment soon
proved inadequate even to cover the purely domestic arrangements. This fact was stressed by the secretary at a meeting of the
trustees on 15th December 1954, when Churchill was the Prime
Minister. The trustees agreed that duality was undesirable and
instructed the secretary to pursue the matter with the Treasury
with a view to the trust controlling the whole estate with the
help of an annual grant in aid. This was the course that was
ultimately decided on, and the new arrangement started as from
1st April 1955, but it did not receive statutory authority until the
second Chequers Estate Act became law in 1958.

In 1956, however, about £20,000 was received from the
Treasury by the trustees by way of grant in aid, and this large
sum was used to modernize completely the interior of Chequers.
Really effective central heating was installed, thus rectifying the
cold in winter of which Harry Hopkins had complained so

bitterly. Wash basins and running water were also laid on in all the bedrooms – it had been one of Churchill's complaints that his guests had to make their way along draughty corridors in the morning to the nearest bathroom to wash their teeth.

By the Statute of 1958, it was enacted that the Treasury might "out of moneys provided by Parliament make grants in aid of the expenses of the (Chequers) Administrative Trustees . . . in the upkeep, repair and maintenance of the mansion house and other buildings and the gardens, pleasure grounds and other lands comprised in the Chequers Estate (including the wages of gardeners and other persons employed in connection therewith)." The Act also made certain changes in the trusteeship. The Prime Minister himself ceased to be a trustee, but Lady Lee remained one.

Since then, substantial grants have been made by the Treasury, and the total annual amount received by the trustees from this source is around £12,000 per annum. This is in addition to the income from the endowment, about £6,000 a year, so that the total expenditure on Chequers is now about £18,000 a year. The amount paid to the Prime Minister for food, etc. still remains at £15 for each weekend, but when he entertains overseas visitors officially, e.g., the members or representatives of other Governments, he can claim the expense of doing so from public funds.

A problem of considerable importance has recently arisen in regard to the woodlands. The Chilterns are renowned for their beautiful trees, and those which surround Chequers are part of a much larger area which has for generations been a source of infinite delight not only to the neighbourhood but also to visitors from other districts and indeed from all over the world. Cobbett's description of this part of the country in the early nineteenth century is well known: "The trees are very fine oaks, ashes and beeches. They are in great numbers and make the fields look most beautiful. No villainous thugs of the fir tribe offend the eye here."

Lee himself was extremely proud of the woodlands and most anxious that their beauty should be preserved. In the original deed he stipulated that "The woods, shrubberies and trees are not to be cleared or cut down but merely thinned, cropped and re-planted from time to time in accordance with the most approved methods of forestry."

But woodlands, however beautiful, need constant attention, and sometimes a lot of money spending on them if they are to retain their beauty and amenity value and not to deteriorate. The beech is not a particularly long-lived tree, and most of those at Chequers are between 100 and 150 years old. In recent years the trustees have been increasingly conscious of this fact and of the mounting expenditure which is likely to have to be incurred on the woods in the future. It is quite true that this expenditure could probably be recovered by grants in aid from the Treasury, but the trustees have been and still are anxious that the taxpayers' bill in this matter should be as low as possible. It was with this in mind that they approached the Forestry Commission; it was ultimately agreed that the Commission should acquire the Chequers woodlands for a sum of about £40,000.

The news of the sale has given rise to widespread anxiety, not only locally but amongst admirers of Chequers and its surroundings everywhere. These fears though natural, are, however, almost certainly groundless. The greatest care has been exercised by the trustees in exacting from the Commission detailed assurances that the full amenities of Chequers will at all times be preserved. They have ascertained that it is not the intention of the Commission to indulge in large scale felling or to replace the beautiful beech trees by "Villainous thugs of the fir tribe". On the contrary, the Commission have made it abundantly clear that the maintenance of the typical characteristics of the landscape will be the overriding consideration. It will probably not be for at least another seventy years that any large-scale replacement of the existing trees will be necessary, and even when this happens there is every reason to suppose that the general character of the woodlands will be changed as little as possible. Meanwhile, at least in the early stages, the aim will be to plant with beech the existing gaps in the woods. Later on, as and when it becomes necessary to cut down some of the older trees, they will be replaced in the main by beech. There are undoubtedly parts of the woods where a certain amount of thinning out will be desirable in order to keep the remaining trees healthy, but it is understood that this will be done in such a way as not to affect the appearance of the woodlands from the distance. Wild cherry is fairly common in the woods at present, and this will be encouraged to grow along with the beech. A small consultative committee will be set up, consisting of certain of the trustees and one or two members of the Commission's conservancy staff and there will be continuous consultation between the two sides about the future management of the woodlands.

It may, of course, be asked what, if the amenities are to be fully preserved and the woodlands not run on a purely commercial basis, is the point of the sale. Does it amount to any more than transferring the expense of maintaining the amenity from one government department to another? The answer to this is that there will be important administrative economies and a great gain in efficiency as a result of the sale to the Forestry Commission, who already own another large area in the district, which, incidentally, they have always managed with a high regard for the local amenities.

Before closing this chapter, which has been concerned almost exclusively with matters of an administrative nature, it is not inappropriate to make mention of the devoted labours of Mr C. F. Penruddock, who has served the trustees as their secretary since 1936 and has also, during the whole of this period, acted as the agent for the Chequers estate, a position which has involved a great deal of work and many intricate problems. Down the years, he has applied himself with unflagging zeal to the place and his efforts have been greatly appreciated by the various Prime Ministers and by Lord and Lady Lee.

15

The Influence of Chequers

IT is now rather over fifty years since Lee made his first gift of Chequers to the nation and rather less than that since, the Lees having relinquished their life interests, the first Prime Minister moved in as tenant. Looking back over this period of half a century we can now attempt an assessment of the success or failure of the scheme which Lee first inaugurated in 1917.

In the main, there can be no doubt that Lee's plan has been an unqualified success, reflecting great credit on the wisdom, imagination and foresight of its author. Chequers has proved to be a great advantage not only to the Prime Ministers and their wives but also to successive governments and to the nation. A more difficult question to answer is how far what may perhaps be described as Lee's subsidiary objectives have been brought to fruition. "To the revolutionary statesman," he wrote, "the antiquity and calm tenacity of Chequers and its annals might suggest some saving virtues in the continuity of English history and exercise a check upon too hasty upheavals. . . ."

How far has this hope been realized? It might, of course, be argued that no one of the Prime Ministers who have so far occupied Chequers (including three Socialists) deserves the title of a "revolutionary statesman". Ramsay MacDonald certainly stood in no need of any mellowing influences. He entered Chequers 'as to the manner born', and from the moment that he first set foot in the place as its master he gave every indication of enormously appreciating not only Chequers itself but what it stood for as well. He did not need Chequers to persuade him of the "saving virtues" inherent in "the continuity of English history". Few men have had a deeper veneration for that continuity with its attendant pageantry than he. In so far as he had any prejudice against rich men or their way of life, it was certainly not towards the ancient aristocracy that such feelings were directed. He adored staying in their houses and gloried in the gracious living that he found there. It was, as he himself said more than once, "the pushing upstart millionaires", "the hard faced men who had done well out of the war" and what he regarded as "vulgar ostentation" that he disliked.

Attlee was utterly different, both in character and personality, from MacDonald. There is little evidence that he was ever particularly attracted to country house life as such. But he was always deeply interested in history, and he had a love of beauty and beautiful surroundings. There was no element of vindictiveness in his composition, and his Socialism was certainly not born of envy, hatred and malice towards those who happened to have more of this world's goods than he had. Rather was it born of a genuine sympathy for and desire to help the least fortunate among his fellow human beings. It is worthy of notice that it was Attlee's government which first made it possible for the owners of historic houses to obtain grants from the government, in certain circumstances, for their repair and maintenance.

Harold Wilson, too, has a strong sense of history and takes great pride in showing his guests round Chequers and telling them something of its past. And it is worth recording that Mrs Wilson twice visited Lady Lee at her flat in the Albany, talking to her about the place, and that Lady Lee greatly appreciated her visits. Lady Douglas Home also went to see her.

Though they have all three undoubtedly enormously appreciated the place, it is, on the whole, unlikely that any one of Labour's three Prime Ministers has been sensibly affected one way or the other by Chequers in their attitude towards other such places and their owners. If Lee's hope was that Chequers would do something to "remove the chip from Socialist shoulders" about country houses and country house life it is unlikely that it has been realized. It must be remembered that Chequers is not and has not for the last fifty years been an ordinary country house. Hounds do not normally meet there, and neither shooting parties nor hunt balls are held there. Only once since it became public property has the place been thrown open to the local hunt and that, appropriately enough, was

Harold Wilson shows Napoleon's dispatch case to President Nixon during the latter's visit to Chequers in February 1969. This is one of a number of Napoleonic relics presented to Chequers by Lord Lee

Two views of Chequers: (*above*) the north front showing the First World War German cannon in the grounds; (*below*) the south front in winter

during the time of Stanley Baldwin. The Prime Minister of the day is not expected to and does not in fact mix with his country neighbours, nor does his wife normally do so, though Mrs Baldwin used occasionally to give a party in the Great Hall to which she invited some of the people who lived locally. In recent years, the atmosphere has become increasingly that of an officers' mess, with Ministers constantly arriving for conferences and their wants being attended to by members of the A.T.S., W.R.N.S. or W.A.A.F. The life led at Chequers is so utterly different from that led at most country houses at the present time that there is no reason why the Prime Minister should be influenced either for or against country house life in general by being there.

But no one with a sense of history could go to Chequers without being keenly interested and stimulated, while at the same time recognizing its great charm and character and the timelessness of the place. Great men have come and gone, great scenes have been enacted, great speeches have been made and prepared there but let the last word rest with the inscription on the old sundial in the south garden:

> Ye houres do flie
> Full soon we die
> In age secure
> Ye house and hills
> Alone endure.

M

Bibliography

Attlee, C. R., *As it Happened* (Heinemann, 1954).

Avon, Earl of, *The Eden Memoirs: Facing the Dictators, Full Circle* (Cassell, 1962).

Baldwin, A. W., *My Father, the True Story* (Allen and Unwin, 1955).

Beaverbrook, Lord, *The Decline and Fall of Lloyd George* (Collins, 1963).

——, *Politicians and the War* (Butterworth, 1928).

Blake, Robert, *The Private Papers of Douglas Haig* (Eyre and Spottiswoode, 1952).

——, *The Unknown Prime Minister : the Life and Times of Andrew Bonar Law* (Eyre and Spottiswoode, 1955).

Boothby, Lord, *My Yesterday, Your Tomorrow* (Hutchinson, 1962).

Broad, Lewis, *Winston Churchill* (Hawthorn Brooks, 1958 and 1963).

Bryant, Arthur, *Stanley Baldwin, a Tribute* (Hamish Hamilton, 1937).

——, *Turn of the Tide: a study based on the Diaries, etc of Field-Marshal Lord Alanbrooke* (Collins, 1957).

——, *Triumph in the West* (Collins, 1959).

Buchan, John, *Oliver Cromwell* (Hodder and Stoughton, 1964).

Butcher, Henry C., *Three Years with Eisenhower* (Heinemann, 1946).

Callwell, Major General Sir C. E., *Field-Marshal Sir Henry Wilson, his Life and Diaries*, 2 Vols. (Cassell, 1927).

Cazalet Keir, Thelma, *From the Wings, an Autobiography* (Bodley Head, 1967).

Childs, Marquis, *Eisenhower, Captive Hero* (Hammond and Hammond, 1959).

Churchill, Randolph, *The Fight for the Tory Leadership* (Heinemann, 1964).

Churchill, Winston S., *History of the Second World War*, 6 Vols. (Cassell, 1948–1954).

——, *War Speeches*, compiled by Charles Eade (Cassell, 1952).

Citrine, Lord, *Men and Work* (Hutchinson, 1966).

Clark, General Mark, *Calculated Risk* (Harrap, 1951).

Cobbett, William, *Rural Rides*.

Collier, Basil, *Leader of the Few: Air Chief Marshal Lord Dowding* (Jarrolds, 1957).

Costello, William, *The Facts about Nixon, a Candid Biography* (Hutchinson, 1960).

Dalton, Hugh, *High Tide and After: Memoirs 1945–1960* (Muller, 1960).

Davis, Richard Herding, *The Cuban and Porto Rican Campaigns* (Heinemann, 1899).

De Gaulle, Charles, *War Memoirs*, translated by Jonathan Griffin (Collins, 1955).

Douglas of Kirtleside, Lord, *Years of Command* (Collins, 1966).

Eisenhower, Dwight D., *Memoirs, Waging Peace, Vol 2: The White House Years 1956–1961* (Heinemann, 1966).

——, *At Ease* (Robert Hale, 1967).

Elletson, D. H., *Roosevelt and Wilson, a Comparative Study* (John Murray, 1965).

——, *The Chamberlains* (John Murray, 1966).

Feiling, Keith, *The Life of Neville Chamberlain* (Macmillan, 1946).

Gunther, John, *Roosevelt in Retrospect* (Hamish Hamilton, 1950).

Haldane, Richard Burdon, *Autobiography* (Hodder and Stoughton, 1929).

Hankey, Lord, *The Supreme Command 1914–1918*, 2 Vols. (Allen and Unwin, 1961).

Harris, Marshal of the R.A.F. Sir Arthur, *Bomber Offensive* (Collins, 1947).

Harrison, Michael, *Mulberry, The Return in Triumph* (W. H. Allen, 1965).

Hart Davis, Rupert, *The Cuban War*.

Historical Manuscripts Commission, *Report on the Manuscripts of Mrs Frankland Russell Astley of Chequers Court, Bucks.*

Ismay, Hastings L., *The Memoirs of General the Lord Ismay* (Heinemann, 1954).

Jenkins, J. Gilbert, *Chequers: a History of the Prime Minister's Buckinghamshire Home* (Pergamon Press, 1967).

Jones, Thomas, *Lloyd George* (Oxford University Press, 1951).

——, *A Diary with Letters 1931–1950* (Oxford University Press, 1954).

——, *Whitehall Diary, Vol I 1916–1925* (Oxford University Press, 1969).

Kennan, George F., *Memoirs 1925–1950* (Hutchinson, 1968).

Kilmuir, Earl, *Memoirs* (Weidenfeld and Nicolson, 1964).

Lipscomb, George, *History and Antiquities of the County of Buckingham* (J. and W. Robins, 1847).

Lloyd George, D., *War Memoirs* (Ivor Nicholson and Watson).

Maisky, Ivan, *Memoirs of a Soviet Ambassador: The War 1939–1943*, translated by A. Rothenstein (Hutchinson, 1967).

Mazo, Earl, and Hess, Stephen, *President Nixon, a Political Portrait* (MacDonald, 1968).

Menzies, Sir Robert Gordon, *Afternoon Light* (Cassell, 1967)

Middlemas, Keith, and Barnes, John, *Baldwin, a Biography* (Weidenfeld and Nicolson, 1969).

Millis, Walter, *The Martial Spirit* (Literary Guild of America, 1931).

Monypenny, W. F., and Buckle, E., *Life of Benjamin Disraeli, Earl of Beaconsfield*, Vol. I (John Murray, 1910).

Nel, Elizabeth, *Mr Churchill's Secretary* (Hodder and Stoughton, 1958).

Nicolson, Harold, *Diaries and Letters 1930–39* (Collins, 1966).

Nixon, Richard M., *Six Crises* (W. H. Allen, 1962).

Normanbrooke, Colville, and others, *Action this Day, Working with Churchill* (Macmillan, 1968).

Nutting, Anthony, *No End of a Lesson: the Story of Suez* (Cassell, 1967).

Owen, Frank, *Tempestuous Journey: Lloyd George, his Life and Times* (Hutchinson, 1954).

Pawle, G., *The War and Colonel Warden* (Harrap, 1963).

Raymond, E. T., *Mr Lloyd George* (Collins, 1922).

Reynolds, Quentin, *By Quentin Reynolds* (Heinemann, 1964).

Rice, Sir Cecil, *Letters and Friendships*, edited by Stephen Gwynn (Houghton Mifflin, 1929).

Roberts, Bechofer, *Stanley Baldwin, Man or Miracle* (Robert Hale, 1936).

Roosevelt, Eleanor, *Autobiography* (Hutchinson, 1962).

Roosevelt, Theodore, *The Rough Riders* (Scribner, 1899).

——, *Letters of*, selected and edited by Elting E. Morison (Harvard University Press, 1951).

Sherwood, Robert E., *The White House Papers of Harry Hopkins*, 2 Vols. (Eyre and Spottiswoode, 1949).

Shorter, C., *Highways and Byways in Buckinghamshire* (Macmillan, 1920).

Smuts, J. C., *Jan Christian Smuts* (Cassell, 1952).

Summersby, Kay, *Eisenhower was My Boss* (Werner Laurie, 1949).

Sylvester, A. J., *The Real Lloyd George* (Cassell, 1929).

Taylor, A. J. P., *Oxford History of England*, Vol XV, 1914–1945 (Clarendon Press, 1965).

Thompson, Walter H., *Assignment Churchill* (Farrar Strauss and Cudeby, 1955).

Vansittart, Lord, *The Mist Procession* (Hutchinson, 1958).

Webb, Beatrice, *Diaries 1924–1932*, edited with an introduction by Margaret Cole (Longmans Green, 1956).

Weir, L. McNeil, *The Tragedy of Ramsay MacDonald* (Secker and Warburg, 1938).

Wright, Robert, *Dowding and the Battle of Britain* (Macdonald, 1969).

Young, G. M., *Stanley Baldwin* (Hart Davis, 1952).

Index